Connecting

Rewire Your Relationship-Culture

Victoria Lorient-Faibish
RP, MEd (Psych), CCC, BCPP, RPP, RPE,
Registered Psychotherapist, Holistic Psychotherapist,
Relationship Expert, Life Coach and Speaker

Foreword by Dini Petty

Library and Archives Canada
Cataloguing in Publication

Lorient-Faibish, Victoria, 1965-, author

Connecting : rewire your relationship culture / Victoria Lorient-Faibish (RP, Med (Psych), CCC, BCPP, RPP, RPE, Registered Psychotherapist, Holistic Psychotherapist, Relationship Expert, Life Coach and Speaker) ;   foreword by Dini Petty.

ISBN 978-1-988058-07-8 (bound).
--ISBN 978-1-988058-06-1 (paperback)

1. Interpersonal relations. 2. Man-woman relationships.
3. Dating (Social customs). 4. Marriage. 5. Self-consciousness (Awareness).   I. Petty, Dini, writer of foreword II. Title.

BF637.C45L69 2016   158.2   C2015-908262-5

Published 2016 by Manor House Publishing Inc. (905)-648-2193
Cover Design/layout/realization: Donovan Davie/ Michael Davie
All rights reserved via publisher/author (Copyright: Author).
Editor: Andrea Lemieux
Creator of connecting people art: Georges Sarkis

We acknowledge the financial support of the Government of Canada through the Canada Book Fund for this project.

Important Disclaimer Note: This publication contains the opinions and ideas of its author. It is intended to provide helpful, informative material on subjects addressed herein. It's sold with the understanding that the author and publisher are not engaged in rendering medical, health or any other kind of personal professional services in the book. The reader should consult his or her medical, health or other competent professional before adopting any of the suggestions in the book or drawing inferences from it. The author and publisher specifically disclaim all responsibility for any liability, loss or risk, personal or otherwise, which is incurred as a consequence, directly or indirectly, of the use or application of any of the contents of this book.

Author's Note: Case studies in this book are amalgams of people and do not pertain to any one person. All names are fictitious and gender and occupation, have been changed to protect the subjects' identities.

I dedicate this book to my husband, Kevin, who is my partner, lover, best friend and unconditional supporter. Life is much sweeter with you. Thank you for your love and care. I love all of you – always.

Contents

Foreword

Connecting: Rewire Your Relationship-Culture is a book I wish had existed when I was starting my journey, way back then.

Like many of us, I come from a dysfunctional family background, and as Victoria points out, "If you do not analyze and process the family-culture in which you grew up, you are doomed to repeat old patterns."

So I stumbled about repeating losing patterns, wondering why it wasn't working. Eventually, while working on Third World aid, I realized that the real miracle would be if I could save myself, and I began the long journey of introspection to free myself and end the cycle of dysfunction in my family.

This book would have made my journey shorter and easier.

It will guide you through your family matrix, into dating in the modern world, how to spot relationship dysfunction from the start and finally lead you into healthy relationships and enduring marriages.

Unraveling your life thorough an introspective journey requires a lot of work, time and commitment: "There is no way around the mountain," but if you wish to transform your life and your relationships, the path lies within these pages. With Victoria Lorient-Faibish as your guide, these treasures are within your reach.

- Dini Petty

Dini Petty is a renowned Canadian television and radio host and the first female traffic reporter to pilot her own helicopter.

Introduction

The Power of Relating

"No man is an island, entire of itself; every man is a piece
of the continent, a part of the main."
~ John Donne, *Devotions upon Emergent Occasions*,
"Meditation XVII"

Knowing oneself fully is paramount to a balanced and
healthy life. To achieve this involves an introspective
journey — diving into the deep waters of self-knowing and
self-awareness, which I covered in depth in my first book,
*Find Your "Self-Culture": Moving from Depression and
Anxiety to Monumental Self-Acceptance.*

As a holistic psychotherapist who works with people every
day as they wander through their dating, relationship,
marriage and family lives, I am compelled to write this
book based on my clinical experience over the last nearly
twenty years. In it, I provide case studies and effective,
simple tools for people to improve and rewire the way they
enter the dance of relating to others in a healthy way.

It is through relating that I feel the richest lessons in life
can occur. It is through connection that the deepest
understanding of self and intimacy can be attained.

But if we do not look at what we inherited from our
families of origin — our "family-culture," we will project
this onto our adult relationships. Our lack of awareness and

our neural pathways associated with our unconscious patterns will lead us to repeat exactly what we saw, and if what we saw was dysfunctional, we will repeat this in our adult lives, perpetuating the cycle of dysfunction into oblivion.

In this book, I speak in depth about how we can rewire our neural pathways and our patterns of behavior so that we can have relationships that are more conscious and healthy and lives that are of our own choosing. Through this process you can, if you choose, rewire your "relationship-culture."

What Is "Relationship-Culture"?

Our relationship-culture lurks in every single one of us.

It is the very matrix of how you react to your dates, relationships, partners or spouses and is reflected in your neural pathways, your reactions, your patterns and your ways of being.

Your relationship-culture is your external expression of your family-culture. If you do not analyze and process the family-culture in which you grew up, you are doomed to repeat old patterns unconsciously.

If you do nothing about any dysfunction carried with you from your family-culture, you have no choice but to play that matrix out in your life and foist it onto the next generation.

Left unanalyzed, your patterns will repeat. How your emotions play out in your relationships, how you behave in your relationships and how your relationships evolve are all a part of your relationship-culture.

The key is to know exactly what your relationship-culture is — the collection of repetitive relationship patterns that may or may not be dysfunctional. Awareness is the key.

Yet awareness alone can do nothing.

More needs to happen for change to occur if change is needed.

If the patterns that you inherited from your family-culture are dysfunctional and negatively impact your relationship-culture, then real change needs to happen lest you perpetuate the cycle of dysfunction in yourself and for generations to come.

In this book, I discuss many ways for a person to do something concrete to effect change in response to any awareness that may arise. To effect real change and to create a new normal, a "rewiring" of the neural pathways associated with the relationship-culture needs to evolve.

To be clear, this is not about throwing everything away that you learned from your family-culture.

Please keep whatever is working and is functional and healthy.

This book is about becoming aware of what is not working with regard to what you inherited from your family-culture so that you can create a new, fully unique, personalized, choice-filled, healthy, mindful relationship-culture that you now, completely and consciously, bring into your adult relationships.

Where It All Starts: Family-Culture

Your family-culture is all you know in the beginning. It influences all aspects of your life. This is something you engage in without thinking. It is something that gives you a sense of community, belonging and family — when it is working for you. When it is not, it may cause you to feel unhappy. It can exert undue pressure on you to conform and fit into what your family knows and has done for generations. Family-culture includes the emotional baggage handed down through generations that profoundly affects the life of any given family.

The relationships, such as between parents and children, brothers and sisters, grandparents and grandchildren, are the real meat of the issue, and from where a family-culture derives. These relationships influence how a person turns out and how they interact in their own adult relationships. The family-culture has a profound effect on your relationship-culture.

What you experienced in your family dynamics growing up is largely what you will replay in your adult relationships.

On the whole, we come from tribes, our families, with unique ways of doing things, and these patterns, habits and ways of communicating and relating are what you have metabolized as your family-culture, and it lives deep within your consciousness.

The unresolved issues, hurts, traumas, family patterns, secrets, shames, triumphs, jealousies, abandonments and fears are all part of your particular family-culture that profoundly inform how you interact in your adult relationships and that infiltrate your relationship-culture.

9

The Attachment Trauma

Simply put, much of what you play out in your adult relationship patterns that is not healthy and happy often stems from an attachment wound or trauma early in life that was never fully processed and resolved. The event or the series of events you metabolized as a trauma still lives in your body and in your consciousness. However, an unconscious drive to understand what happened lies within your psyche. This drive becomes a pattern that you repeat unconsciously in a bid to shed awareness on it so that you can fully understand what occurred.

This wound or trauma could have happened in your family of origin during your early life experiences.

You may have felt abandoned, possibly by your dad or your mom or your siblings, which then may have translated into neediness, overcontrol, codependency, anxiety, defensiveness, overprotectiveness and so much more. What occurred in your young years outside of your family-culture also impacts you profoundly. You may have been bullied as a child at school, and this turned into a maladjustment in the way you relate to other people and social anxiety that creates overselfcriticism and an internal self-bullying dialogue.

Or, it caused you to become overprotective of yourself so that your walls are too big to allow intimacy and deep connection. I have observed people who had the unfortunate experience of having acne when they were teenagers, and this became a trauma that haunted them into their adulthood, even though their skin had cleared up completely. They always felt as though they had to hide, and it impacted how they related to others, especially as they were trying to date and form connections in that realm.

Healing the Attachment Trauma

Healing the attachment trauma requires looking at the trauma quite directly. Remembering the events, talking about the events and sharing the events with a trusted and safe person all contribute to a person's being able to reframe the events that occurred during childhood.

When we look gently yet directly at the trauma and set up an environment, through visualization, in which the "hurt child" within is made to feel safe, seen and honored, we are able to promote healing.

I encourage clients to visualize their bringing forth an aspect of their adult selves that feels confident, and to see themselves protecting the hurt child, while at the same time remembering the traumatic event or events.

Sometimes I ask clients to also imagine a protective being or animal to be part of this visualization. For example, they visualize a very strong and powerful tiger or bear to accompany them.

This visualization is a therapeutic process and is part of the reframing of the trauma, where the child felt completely powerless. With this kind of visualization and support, we are able to diminish the power that the trauma has had over them. And since the brain responds very well to visualization because it does not distinguish between what is real and what is imagined, this therapeutic process helps to heal the attachment trauma.

The visualization and the reframing process encourage the brain to set up new neural pathways and encourage the biochemistry of ease and calm versus fear and trauma.

Thus, where once a person felt victimized by the events, reframing them now helps the person to see them with new eyes from the perspective of the adult, where they now feel they have more power and more choice.

They no longer need to be at the mercy of the past, and the trauma no longer needs to dominate them. Yes, the trauma did occur and the attachment trauma did have an impact, but the person is able to leave it firmly in the past so that it isn't constantly informing the present and the future.

Feeling supported and relaxed while recounting the events that were traumatic in the past goes a long way toward removing the power and the charge that the trauma once had. The sharing process also helps diminish the fear and the shame. The process of reframing the past gives a person the opportunity to make new choices and to develop a new experience regarding connections, attachments and relationships in general. This helps a person to rewire their relationship-culture quite significantly.

Without reframing the trauma, without this kind of awareness, a person often allows the fear and anxiety that the event or events created to color their relationships into adulthood, and possibly forever.

One thing I do want to mention is that we are doomed to repeat what we do not adequately and completely understand and process. People tend to attract toward themselves the same types of people they encountered in their family of origin that created the original attachment trauma. So it is very important that, when you bring people into your life to date and have relationships with, you make sure you are not constantly retriggering the attachment trauma, scratching the attachment trauma "scab" as it were, that you are trying to heal. For example, I recommend not allowing a person who is constantly elusive, moody, aloof and unreliable into your life if you don't want to constantly retrigger the abandonment trauma. Similarly, I encourage people who came from violent and abusive environments to work diligently to not bring more of the same into their relationships, even though it may feel normal — and even attractive — at times.

Neural Pathways: Doing Things Over and Over

Doing the same thing over and over and expecting a different result is a funny definition of madness that I love and often use because it speaks to the core of why, in my opinion, people suffer through painful, repetitive patterns in their lives and relationships.

But like the frog that doesn't know it will boil to death when placed in a pot of cold water that is put atop a hot burner, people don't know they are in a kind of self-destructive madness when they blindly repeat the same actions and travel the same emotional and relationship trajectories as they go through their lives in a semi-autopilot way.

And, to make matters more challenging, accompanying these repetitive actions is the biology of neural pathways in our brain matrix that reinforces this repetition, unless we consciously interrupt the duplication. In his book *The Brain That Changes Itself: Stories of Personal Triumph from the Frontiers of Brain Science*, Norman Doidge explains that our brains reinforce the neural pathways with each repetitive behavior and belief.

The more we do the same thing, the more the neural pathway associated with that repetition strengthens. The longer that belief remains in place or action continues, the more that neural pathway is reinforced. But this process also works brilliantly in our favor if change is desired.

Our brains are elegantly adaptable. If you decide to behave differently in your dating experiences or in a relationship, although it will feel uncomfortable and strange at first, your brain will collaborate and support the new behavior by creating new neural pathways.

If you consciously repeat the new behavior often, these new neural pathways will be reinforced, thus allowing your biology to help you to stay the course with the new choices. This is the way to change the patterns that no longer work for you. The key is to identify what you are doing and where it all started, and then determine if it is working for you. If it is not, then find a new pattern of behavior and repeat, repeat, repeat!

In this book I share information about what it means to repeat patterns that are dysfunctional, unhealthy and unconscious. Through this awareness I share information as to the process of rewiring the way a person relates to others in the realms of dating, relationships, marriage and divorce.

If you no longer want to repeat dysfunctional cycles, then this is the book for you! If you want to create new neural pathways that correspond with new behaviors with respect to the way you relate in your adult relationships, you are essentially saying you would like to rewire your relationship-culture, which will positively impact your future generations.

This is an opportunity for you to become truly aware of what no longer works for you so that you can then proceed to rewiring your relationship-culture!

Part I

Dating in the Modern World

"Before you enter the dating pool, mine your feelings profoundly. Ask the key questions of yourself: Why do I react the way I do? What do I want? What don't I want? In what kind of situation do I feel most safe? And why? How do I thrive in a relationship? What are my triggers? What is my go-to pattern of behavior when I'm in a relationship?"
- Victoria Lorient-Faibish

Chapter 1

Know Yourself

When you decide to enter the dating world in a healthy way, it is most important to make sure you first get in touch with your innate, authentic self. The more conscious you are of who you are, the more likely you are to attract someone who is best suited to you.

Watch out for living in your "false self." Making decisions from your false self leads to poor decisions. This planet needs your authenticity. Know yourself.

Avoid going down the rabbit hole of denial. If you got messaging from your family of origin that you are not a good enough person, or that relationships and people are dangerous, that is what you will bring to your world — your dating world, and that may actually not be your real self, but simply a personality that evolved as a result of your upbringing!

Ask yourself deep questions. Keep a journal.

Before you enter the dating pool, mine your feelings profoundly. Ask the key questions of yourself: Why do I react the way I do? What do I want? What don't I want? In what kind of situation do I feel most safe? And why? How do I thrive in a relationship? What are my triggers? What is my go-to pattern of behavior when I am in a relationship?

Get to know yourself. Get to know your self-culture. My first book, *Find Your "Self-Culture,"* explores this subject in depth. I feel that finding your self-culture is most important as you navigate through your relationship experiences to live from the viewpoint of a clear self-knowing, in which the loudest voice in your head, guiding your every move and decision, comes from a strong self-culture. The more conscious you are of who you are, the more likely you are to attract someone toward you who suits you best.

Living from the False Self

We cannot change what we are not aware of. We are doomed to repeat over and over anything we are unconscious of.

I feel that meditation and introspection are crucial to one's relationship to one's self as it encourages deep self-awareness. If you are living in deep lack of awareness of why you engage in relationships the way you do, you need to go about the business of navigating in depth who you are so that when you enter the dating world and an eventual relationship, you are not simply repeating dysfunctional patterns you learned from your family-culture or your childhood experiences.

The false self usually develops as a way of surviving and coping with what was observed and experienced in the family-culture. This is the self that evolved quite naturally and unconsciously to fit in with the tribe you came from, whether it was healthy or not. This is what you observed early on and took on as part of the matrix of your personality style. To be clear, this is not your authentic self — your self-culture. This is the false self.

There are many versions of what the false self may be, but all of them contribute to how you interact in your adult

18

relationships, and, over time, it is largely an untenable way to conduct a happy, healthy and mature life. For example (and this is just one example of what you might unconsciously be bringing forth), your family-culture might have taught you that it's important to please everybody. This is not your real self; it is the self that evolved in order to cope. Feeling that pleasing everyone is the only way to keep the peace is what you were taught. I call this the "disease-to-please." If you were taught this pattern of behavior, it is likely that you are largely unconscious of it as it would have become an instinctual way of being.

When a person lives with the disease-to-please, and because it is so difficult to maintain, the pattern will surely land the person in deep resentment and depression, and, over time, this trait is not sustainable. And if this is what you bring to the dating scene or a relationship, you are sure to choose people whom you are looking to take care of and to please as you have normalized this patterning. This creates an imbalance in the dynamic and will land you feeling trapped in an unhealthy relationship-culture dynamic.

Case Study: Living from the False Self

Susan kept falling for men who were not available. Either they were attached or just not emotionally equipped for intimacy. This pattern seemed like an addiction that she could not break. These men were like crack cocaine to her.

What really sparked her interest was a good old-fashioned married guy who was looking to cheat on his wife. The kind who hid his wedding ring when he was at a bar, and even though there was a tan line that indicated there used to be a ring there, that key detail seemed to conveniently go into Susan's denial vault every time. She said that she found all single and available men to be boring. They were not broken enough and not nearly interesting enough for her. She came in to see me because she found herself suffering deeply from guilt and, finally, a deep desire to break this cycle of dysfunction that was clearly an emotional hangover from her attachment wound from her experience in her family of origin.

As we started her therapy, she began to reveal her parents' turmoil-filled marriage. They stayed together for many years, but it was clear they were not happy. She said that as a child she used to be woken up by the loud voices of her fighting parents. Her dad, a drinker, would take to fits of rage, and her mother was the soother, the victim who put up with him no matter what. Susan would sit on the floor in the dark by her bedroom door, listening to the sordid content of their fights.

She would sometimes quietly tiptoe to the landing of the stairs to watch them, and she would catch a glimpse of her mother as she said things like, "You can't leave us. What will happen to me and the girls? She can't be as important to you as we are." And her dad would come back with comments like, "I need to be free from all this. I'm sick and tired of this life." He was clearly drunk, slurring his words and stumbling about.

Susan remembered registering a feeling of combined disgust, deep hurt and abandonment all mixed in with intrigue. What was so interesting to her father outside the family? Who were these women he preferred to be with? What did they have that her mother didn't have? Then, as time went on, her relationship with her mother suffered profoundly as Susan found herself blaming her mother for being uninteresting, dependent and not compelling enough to keep her father from cheating. She vowed to herself that she would not be like her mother when she grew up. She became fiercely independent in her career and her finances, and she evolved emotionally into a person who was so self-sufficient that she never asked for help. She never exposed her weaknesses. Very few people knew who the real Susan was. She didn't really know herself either.

She didn't know it until later, when she did some deep emotional investigating, but she was subconsciously trying to become the kind of woman her father would like, find interesting, love and not abandon. This realization was positively jaw-dropping to her as it totally resonated with her. It was a watershed moment for her. Somewhere deep inside she had known this about herself, but it had remained buried in her subconscious. Yet this was the unconscious motivating pattern she was repeating over and over. This is what was really impacting who she was and what she was attracted to, as well as what she was attracting toward herself.

Our work did a kind of dismantling of the very matrix that motivated her. Once she had the awareness, she could not un-ring that bell of awareness. Together we did some deep self-esteem work, in which she was able to develop a clearer sense of her own values and boundaries. She was able to neutralize the aspects of herself that were driven by that kind of excitement. Eventually, she no longer needed the excitement to feel alive.

In real terms, the building of one's self-esteem occurs when we set a small goal, and, with diligence, we are able to achieve that goal, and then we are able to celebrate our accomplishment. I asked Susan to treat this old behavior like an addiction that she needed to gain sobriety from. I asked her to work with her lack of comfort and with the pain that would arise when she didn't give into the old pattern of behavior. This was not in the slightest way easy for her. But with each day of her sobriety from the old ways of being, something started to change in her as the shame started to fall away. She began to like herself a little more because she felt proud of her accomplishment of not giving in. I asked her to start to really focus on what she loved and what her passions might be. She began to derive a sense of aliveness and meaning from her connection to herself and her passions.

With the process of introspective therapy, her parents' story no longer motivated her, and she started to define her own story. She no longer wanted to reinforce the pattern that she had been engaging in as a result of the attachment wound/trauma that had been formed and motivated by the experience of her father being unfaithful to her mother.

She wanted to be free of the shame and guilt that kept creeping in every time she engaged in her past relationship-culture. She needed to rewire her way of being in her adult relationships; she needed to rewire her relationship-culture. Therapy was helping her make that happen. Her feelings of abandonment and resentment did not go away immediately, but she resolved to deal with them in very different ways.

Susan committed to no longer allowing herself to be involved with married men. She went through a kind of detox to help her break this addiction.

Together we worked on her fears around opening herself to single and available men who once had made her run at the very thought that she could fall for and be invested in any of them. Whenever fears show up, it is very important to look at the fear head on. This process is similar to what Dorothy in *The Wizard of Oz* did. She pulled back the curtain on what she thought to be the great and powerful Oz. When Dorothy discovered that what was behind the curtain was simply a small and frail old man instead of a monster that was extremely scary, fear could no longer paralyze her. And this is what happened for Susan.

With baby steps, Susan was able to begin a process of confronting her fears of being hurt that had made her choose to live a life of emotional overprotection. That meant opening herself up to real connection and possible commitment, which had been profoundly scary to her. This was the emotional risk she had been avoiding all her life. She realized her deep fear of abandonment would be truly healed only through the process of improving her relationship with herself. She needed to look inward not outward.

She worked on developing a deeper relationship with her passions as a way to feel more connected to herself so that she did not need to have dysfunctional relationships to feel alive and connected. She started to volunteer at a women's shelter. The act of helping others slowly healed her heart.

The old pattern dissolved as she replaced it with more positive connections to herself and others. She no longer felt shame and guilt. She no longer felt she needed to hide. She became much more open to developing healthy and intimate friendships with other women as well, which became a real source of joy and connection for her.

She made peace with both her parents by developing a sense of compassion and understanding that they had both come from damaged family-cultures as well. Her father had joined AA years before, which had truly transformed the way he interrelated with his family.

After not dating for a time, she was able to go back into the dating world with different motivations and a whole new outlook that allowed her to be attracted to single and available men who sparked her interest and kept her engaged without the emotional hangover traumas from the past. She was no longer living from her false self because she had the courage and did the work to allow her real self to come through.

Every awareness, every session and every new decision and experience rewired her neural pathways and her whole relationship-culture. The metamorphosis had occurred, and Susan reinforced her new normal with each choice and each encounter.

I gave Susan a visualization exercise that greatly helped her increase her self-esteem so that she could consistently keep at bay her false self, which was driven by low self-esteem. I encourage you do the same exercise often (see appendix A, "Visualization to Increase Self-Esteem"). It will help you to keep those associated neural pathways alive and keep you more grounded as you navigate the dating world.

The Chameleon

Another pattern of behavior that I observe in people is that of the chameleon, an animal that can change its color to blend into its environment and provide safety through camouflage. Chameleon behavior in people is when they transform themselves into whatever is necessary to get approval and love and have a sense of belonging. It can be a useful trait in certain circumstances, but it should not be used indiscriminately.

It is important that you not become this chameleon, who simply reflects what is in your environment, because that can eventually wear you out. I observe that people who, after years of doing this, end up feeling depressed and disconnected from their core selves. They have, in effect, stunted the development of their self-culture. I encourage people to be brave and to be themselves. This is the only way to attract back to you the kind of person who fits with you.

Case Study: The Chameleon
Jack was in his thirties and had had a lot of success in corporate sales. He came from a traditional business-minded, self-made family-culture. His parents were demanding and tended to be overcritical. In his home, relaxing was seen as wasteful time that would be better spent working. They were a proud family of entrepreneurs who did not tolerate idle time.

Jack's mother watched his every move and was right on him if he dared to sit and watch TV or simply lie about the house. He loved to draw, but that was seen as a waste of time that he should be using more productively, such as sweeping the family-business store or cleaning his room.

Playing, creating and daydreaming were not okay. Yet it was these very activities that would have helped Jack build a strong sense of trust in himself and in relationships. Playing and creating develop aspects of the brain that foster good development in socialization, healthy attachment and self-trust.[1]

To cope with all this, Jack squashed his true nature and became whatever was needed to fit the environment or situation. He suffered from crippling fear of and guilt for causing others any kind of discomfort or pain, so he constantly went about the business of anticipating what his

---

[1] Joan Packer Isenberg and Mary Renck Jalongo, *Creative Expressions and Play in Early Childhood*, 3rd ed. (New York: Prentice-Hall, 2001).

parents and others needed. He was the perfect child. This continued in a big way into his adult life.

He negotiated the world with his "tentacles" way out, "feeling" the situation, sensing what others needed or if there was danger. If his dad came home from the family store tired and in a bad mood, he made sure he became as quiet as a mouse so as not to incur his wrath. He muted his own personality at every turn.

Later in life, these traits helped him to be successful at work since he had the keen ability to emulate the client, which made them feel comfortable with him. If his client had an interest in wine, he made sure he became a near expert in the topic. He went out of his way to please the clients and to make them feel as if they were doing a deal with a kindred spirit.

This trait would have remained useful if it had not extended into his adult dating and relationship life, which created his relationship-culture.

By the time he came into my office, he was feeling a sense of profound dissatisfaction with life and sadness as well as social anxiety. He felt burned out and even depressed.

This chameleon behavior that he had learned very early in life had caused his authentic self to be completely stunted.

His life had turned into a series of events that were all about being outwardly focused, seeking approval and doing what others needed. All spontaneity and sense of play were gone. These very aspects, which are so crucial to successful dating and letting others know the real you, were not there at all for Jack.

This chameleon pattern makes a person constantly ask questions such as, "Do others love me?" "Am I accepted here?" and "What do I need to do to belong and to please them?" This is too outwardly focused. There is no sense of "What do I need?" "Who am I?" "What makes me happy?" This chips away at your authentic self, which you need to shine through as you make choices when dating and choosing partners and lovers.

Jack and I worked together to bring back his sense of play and creativity as well as his sense of who he really was. He started to write in a journal to keep track of his thoughts and feelings, which helped him to acknowledge himself and hear his inner yearnings and intuition.

For the first time in his life he was listening to himself. The more he listened to himself the better he felt and the more joyful he became. He unearthed a deep longing from his childhood to create art and to play. The more he allowed himself to play, the more his real personality shone through. He joined an improvisational class that let him laugh and try on different ways of being. He discovered that he did not want to throw away the baby with the bath water. His chameleon pattern had created success for him, but he needed to limit it to his work life and to make sure he did not allow it to bleed into his personal life.

This was a great relief for Jack. He finally felt free to date women who were a better match for him, and he allowed himself to say 'no' more often and to say 'yes' only when he truly wanted to. This process helped him to rewire his reactions so that they came from a deep, authentic place within him. He slowly began to rewire his relationship-culture so that the way he was in his adult relationships was vastly different from what he learned during childhood.

If you detect the chameleon pattern in yourself, I suggest that you begin with daily journaling. This is an important place to start because it helps you to "hear" your deepest inner thoughts and yearnings. Acknowledging yourself in this way has the profound effect of interrupting the autopilot chameleon behavior. It allows you to stop and listen carefully to your inner voice and your inner truth.

Find a trusted friend or therapist to share this with. The process of self-acknowledgment, along with sharing it with a non-judgmental and encouraging witness, will help you to feel more open to begin making choices that are different.

Eventually, a new normal will occur, and the chameleon pattern will slip out of your unconscious realm and into deep awareness, where you will allow it to make its presence known only in areas of your life where it can be useful, like Jack, who was able to capitalize on the chameleon pattern at the office.

More False-Self Behavior

Another example of living from the false self is never admitting you're angry, sad or have a problem. We are often taught culturally and societally to squash our feelings, be nice, get along, but it is so important to find a safe space to be authentic, at least with a therapist or a trusted friend. If you don't give your authentic self the time and space to make its presence known, your false self will take over.

Again, I urge you, if you are not able to share authentically with someone, write in a journal and pour your true feelings into it. Get to know what your true feelings about anything are. If you are always in the disease-to-please mode, never admitting you have a problem or an issue, you will develop deep resentment, and anger will show up in various passive-aggressive ways. I have seen this behavior lead to depression, anxiety, dissatisfaction and unhappiness, which, in turn, is a terrible place to come from when you are trying to date and create new relationships.

As adults, the above-mentioned false-self behavior continues, and then in the adult relationships the pattern of being very out of touch with oneself repeats itself to the point of never knowing one's own limits and boundaries. These people are then constantly putting themselves in situations that allow their core beings to be violated. As a result, they feel deeply betrayed, and this often turns into resentment and evolves into manipulative, overreactive behavior that leads to much conflict in their relationships.

The pattern shows up because the person was never taught love can be unconditional and available at all times if they choose. *They* can replenish the profound sense of self-love by giving themselves what *they* need by filling *their own* cups first and giving to others only from the overflow. If they don't understand this, they end up feeling they cannot relax and just be themselves. Their inner-child's sense of "okayness" and self-esteem rises and falls according to how they feel they are being perceived or treated.

If the parents are unreasonably and harshly critical, their children will metabolize the criticism, and to get love and feel they belong, they will turn themselves into whatever is necessary to feel heard, seen and loved by the only group they know — their family and, specifically, their parents.

In many cases, they will stifle their self-expression to achieve this, and they will create a false self that will then inform their relationship-culture later on in life.

Pay Attention: Everyone Is a Mirror

When you go out into the dating scene, be it electronically or face to face, it is wise to remember that you are an energetic being with a measurable vibrational frequency. It is widely understood that thoughts alter your vibrational frequency, which is measured in megahertz, and positive thinking raises your vibration, whereas negative thinking lowers it.

We also know the Law of Attraction, which states that "like attracts like." Thus, your vibrational frequency determines what you attract toward yourself.

If your inner running commentary is oriented toward worst-case scenarios, you'll be more likely to attract negative events and states of being. Therefore, it's a good idea to know what your inner commentary is. I'm talking about those deep inner thoughts that show up in an autopilot way. Your subconscious inner running dialogue, often filled with negativity, is the impactful stuff that may be messing up what you're attracting back toward yourself. It's important you work consistently to become aware of all this.

Each thought, feeling, pattern and emotion you have impacts your vibration, which is like a beacon of energy that you send out, sometimes hurl out, into the universe. This energy then reverberates outward, and all those who match that vibratory frequency will be drawn to this beacon. If you don't know that this dynamic with the universe exists, you will not be able to learn from it. Know that everyone who comes into your field of energy is a mirror to you and your patterns. Even if you are not conscious of the pattern, the person you attract is like a teacher who will give you a tutorial of sorts on the person you are. They will mirror patterns that *you* need to look at within *yourself*. They will show *you* unresolved issues that live within *you*. I invite you to be a keen observer of what and who is in your life. Are those people flaky, jealous, present, absent, consistent, erratic, loving, judgmental, clingy? These are all patterns that may be living inside of you. Instead of criticizing the other person, see the pattern that you observe in the other person as an opportunity to heal or work with inside yourself.

Observe what you see in them and verify if you see it in yourself. Once aware of the pattern you observe in yourself, go about the business of bringing it into balance with therapy, meditation, coaching or some other effective means of transformation. This is the only way to make sure you are not repeatedly attracting toward yourself the same people with the same patterns.

What you put out to the world is what you bring back to you. Yes, there are random occurrences that you do not have control over. But the one thing that you do have a measure of control over is what you are putting out into the world; know that what you put out there does impact what comes back to you. "Like attracts like."

We Teach People How to Treat Us

Remember that at any given moment we are teaching people how to treat us, and this impacts our relationship-culture. Look at how you treat yourself, and that is what you are teaching others about how to treat you. Also, at every turn in a relationship, we teach people what is acceptable or not in our dealings with them. Being aware of the dynamics you allow with friends, partners, casual dates, family, bosses and co-workers is extremely important.

I observe that so many people feel mistreated, victimized, berated and belittled by a variety of people in their lives. In

31

relationships, they habitually permit disrespectful, boundaryless behavior, or they allow others to take advantage of them. I encourage everyone to analyze themselves and their relationships to see how they have essentially taught others — trained them — to think that it is okay to step on their toes, invade their boundaries and not treat them with respect.

If you are in a relationship in which you feel you are being taken advantage of, or belittled or invaded, you need to take responsibility for having somehow trained the other person to treat you that way. If it is repetitive, you have in effect permitted the behavior. You are not the victim, and you cannot blame someone else. Take back your power. Take back your strength and sense of self-loyalty and assert your boundaries. This is a bona fide example of rewiring your relationship-culture.

Tell people what's okay and what isn't. Advise people in a gentle, kind, loving way that it is not okay to treat you with disrespect or belittle or humiliate you. If people are treating you this way, and you're not calling them on it, you need to analyze why you're unable to stand up to them and create courage to tell them where you are at. You have that right!

Getting in "Right Relationship" with Yourself

Getting in "right relationship" with yourself means that you are taking personal responsibility for yourself in all ways. You are not living from the view of a victim. Instead, you are going about the business of becoming emotionally, spiritually and physically fit as a way to prepare your soul, your being, for the dating and relationship experience. Getting in right relationship with yourself means going on a journey to find your "self-culture." Anthropologist Edward Burnett Tylor wrote that culture is "that complex whole which includes knowledge, belief, art, morals, law, custom, and any other capabilities and habits acquired by man as a member of society."[2]

Culture is the full range of learned human behavior patterns, such as ritual, habits and customs. Culture is a powerful tool for survival, but it is a fragile phenomenon, constantly changing and easily lost because it exists only in our minds. And so, self-culture is a collection of personal habits that emanate from a profound knowledge of being deeply in touch with the real you. *It is personalized self-care.* This is the aspect of yourself that may be in hiding due to family-culture pressure to fit in with the tribe.

We comply so as to survive and feel a sense of belonging. However, I observe many who go about life without really getting in touch with their true innate selves, and then they go into the dating and relationship world and wind up feeling out of touch with themselves. They are overly compliant with other people's wants and needs and numbed out to their own needs with a sense of deep dissatisfaction that is projected onto their dates and partners.

"Selfy" versus Selfish

When I started writing my first book, the new word that came on the scene was *selfie*. My made-up word is *selfy*, spelled with a *y*. In my first book, I mention the difference between *selfy* and *selfish*, and I feel it bears repeating here with regard to connecting and relationships.

I like the made-up word *selfy* instead of *selfish*, which means being concerned only with advantages for oneself without regard for others. You may feel that pursuing your

---

[2] Edward Burnett Tylor, *Primitive Culture: Researches into the Development of Mythology, Philosophy, Religion, Art, and Custom,* Vol. 1 (London: John Murray, 1871), 1.

self-culture will make you appear to be mean, selfish and unkind. Yes, the journey does involve *you*; however, you cannot help others unless you are filled with vitality yourself, and so I encourage an attitude of "selfyness."

Selfyness involves the consistent act of listening deeply to your true inner voice and allowing it to be louder than all other voices or opinions. Unless you focus on yourself first, your attempts to give to others from an empty vessel will inevitably result in burnout.

This requires that you know yourself intimately and have a process to continue that dialogue with yourself. You've got to know what you want and need; you cannot have a good and healthy relationship-culture — a relationship with someone else — if your relationship with yourself is off the rails. You can nurture a relationship with yourself only by taking time and slowing it down.

Stop living in autopilot! If you don't know who you are, essentially you are going to make poor choices for yourself, and you will operate from an unconscious place that will create problems in your relationships and your relationship-culture.

As people go about the process of finding their own authentic and unique self-culture, the question that is so often posed to me is whether or not this is a selfish or narcissistic pursuit. This question has usually come from a person who has been shown and trained that to operate from the instinct of self-culture is not a good idea and it is not safe. Trauma and fear arise in them at the very thought of giving themselves permission to claim their self-culture. But being "selfy" does eventually prepare you to be of service to others and to the planet and helps you to do it from a healthy and unresentful perspective. Ultimately, "selfyness" is about community, good relationships and fellowship but from a perspective of filling your own cup first and giving to others only from the overflow.

Finding one's self-culture and being selfy is essential if you are to live a life in which you feel you matter and are in "right" relationship with yourself and others. Also selfishness, which is very different from selfyness, is when you have absolutely no regard whatsoever about the other person and are blind to anyone else but self. With selfyness, there can at times be a conflict of needs, and sometimes a negotiation does have to occur.

But at the core, a person who is selfy is operating from a fair place, where, as they initially try to claim their selfhood, may come off as overly territorial about what they need and want, but, over time, as a deeper comfort around being selfy occurs, people tend to communicate in a more fair, kind, loving way, to which others are receptive. This is especially true if it means that a reciprocity – that nurtures everyone's prerogative in the relationship to claim their self-culture and engage in selfyness – can occur, whether it be casual dating or otherwise.

What Are Your Motivations?

When entering the dating world, it is important to know what your inner motivations are. Sometimes your family-culture can be of a type that has you entering your dating world with a major chip on your shoulder that motivates you to want to overly protect yourself from intimacy. Or, if you have felt emotionally abandoned, you may be anxious in a way that makes you overly needy, and you may subconsciously be looking to be rescued. Or if all you learned from your family tribe was abusive behavior, you may be willing to accept and allow such behavior and less-than-healthy dynamics in your dating experiences.

Many incarnations of this concept can shape the motivations of each person, and one person may have many motivations. Regardless, it is paramount to understand and become intimately familiar with your inner motivations as they do impact your ability to navigate the dating world in an emotionally healthy and empowered way.

Case Study: Balancing the Masculine and Feminine
Max was an attractive woman in her mid-thirties who traveled far and wide in her career as a corporate executive. She came from a family of overachievers who often hit below the belt in an emotional sense when it came to conflict. It simply was not safe to be soft, vulnerable or sensitive. She learned early in life that being vulnerable was tantamount to being weak.

Tapping into the feminine principles of creativity, receptivity and flexibility were not a good idea lest she be completely annulled. This aspect of her personality was frozen in time since she was ten years old. At that age she discovered that to survive she needed to develop a strong personality that would help her navigate her family-culture, and this would later serve her so that she could thrive in the corporate culture.

She loved her job and painstakingly rose to the top of her field. She was respected and well regarded. However, one of the issues she came to see me about was her persistent trouble with men in her dating world and her deep loneliness. She wanted to date and to find a partner, but she kept meeting men whom she liked initially, but then somehow it all fell apart. She had trouble staying interested, and the men also did not stay interested for long.

Max had a deep desire to marry and have children, and as her proverbial biological clock started to tick louder, this issue bubbled up to the surface in a real way.

What were her core issues that influenced the outcomes in her life? As we explored deeper, we found out that the motivations that influenced her external messaging were confused. In the therapy process, we discovered that Max was deeply uncomfortable with exposing her softer side — her vulnerable side — due to her above-mentioned family-culture dynamics. She had built a whole career based on her ability to be strong, direct and clear.

Her "solutioner," alpha-female take-charge way of being had helped her immensely through her professional life, but in her personal life it had been out of balance and had impacted her dating life. She was putting out very confusing messaging to her dates.

We discovered that her inner motivations included wanting to be pampered, pursued and taken care of, not financially, but emotionally. She wanted to be able to be heard and seen and immensely comforted by her prospective partner.

In one session she said in exasperation, "I am exhausted and I need someone to lean on." But when someone did try and provide emotional support, pampering and generally treating her with that kind of attention, Max became anxious and felt boxed in, and she started to find ways to pick apart the person. They never made it past dating. She realized through our sessions that she was not delivering a consistent, conscious message to her prospective dates.

There was a lack of balance in her life and in her motivations, and the messages she was giving out were confusing. Her inner covert motivation was to engage in a committed relationship, yet the very thing that was necessary to becoming more serious with someone she met, that is, exposing her real non-professional self, was locked away, frozen and undeveloped.

She had no idea how to tap into the deeper feminine principle in a healthy way that would allow her to be more receptive and more open to engaging in a softer, less-in-control way of being. She allowed the male aspect of her personality, which had kept her in very good stead at the office, to bleed through into her dating pursuits. Although each and every one of us, male and female, have both masculine and feminine energies within our inner-core beings and our personalities, there is a great need to balance both of these very important aspects.

In Max, this dance between the masculine and the feminine were completely out of balance. Her preconceived notions about tapping into the feminine side led her to erroneously believe one has to lose power, be weak and be lacking boundaries. So she clumsily navigated this aspect, was unsuccessful, and abandoned it completely. It made sense to me that Max would not feel safe tapping into her feminine side because of what she *thought* it meant. But true feminine energy could not be further from her skewed concept. The men she met never really got to know the real Max because Max didn't really know her real self either. To attract the ideal partner, one needs to know oneself deeply and intimately to be able to send out a clear message and energy that is mirrored back to those you attract.

For Max, her messaging was confusing and her dates responded only to her outer personae. Many of these men could not handle her directness or her strength. Others found her too "standoffish" and cold. Ultimately, the trajectory of her dating relationships ended up either with

38

the men rejecting Max – or Max losing interest and rejecting the men. Max was also frustrated and could not understand why there was an imbalance in the communication. She would say, "They don't call!" yet they were very receptive when Max called them.

Max gravitated to being in control, and she found herself to be the one who set the tone and the pace of the relationship. This was familiar and comfortable for her, but she was doing all the work, and she pined to have a man take the lead in her personal world. However, when a man did this, it made her feel like heading for the hills.

Also, the men she met were rarely as successful as Max was, and that eventually became a problem. Some were intimidated by her financial success.

Max initially claimed that this was not a problem for her, but that perspective shifted the deeper the therapy process went. Max needed to correct a deep imbalance to have success in her dating experiences and eventual relationships. To get her motivations and external messaging clearer, we went through a process of helping her redefine what it means to tap into her feminine energy and power.

Feminine energy is not about being subservient or disempowered. It is about being receptive, open, creative, comfortable in your own skin, safe in your vulnerability and emotions, yet having boundaries as part of the mix. It also means liking and respecting yourself.

I asked Max to begin to engage in any activity that required her to tap into her intuition, her creativity, her emotions and her body. It was through this, rather than her overly cerebral engagement, that helped her begin to balance her feminine and masculine sides.

I suggested she take up yoga to start with, and then dance. However, not just any dance class, but improvisational dance instead, which encouraged less control and more inner intuitive movement.

She needed to feel freer in her body. I asked her to play music when she was at home doing activities, such as tidying up or doing laundry. I encouraged her to allow herself to be moved by lovely music, art, dance and anything else that made her soul open up. We engaged in art therapy while listening to flowing and emotional music, whereby I asked her to draw and paint without boundaries or restrictions. I made space to spread out on my office floor and put out crayons, markers, colorful stickers and large pieces paper to draw on.

Initially, she balked at this process. She was out of her element and out of her comfort zone. Yet it was at the very edge of her comfort zone that the growing, the learning and the transforming began for Max. The process helped her to get to know how she truly felt about herself and what she wanted. She started to redefine all of her notions of what it meant to be a woman.

For Max, creating a balance between her masculine and feminine aspects helped her become clear about her motivations in dating. She was able to clarify for herself that she wanted a man who had a career and a life of his own but was comfortable with her powerful, successful side. She was also more comfortable being receptive and open to being wooed and exposing her more vulnerable, softer side. There was now potential for equality and reciprocity in her dating and relationship experiences.

Soon after her deep-therapy sojourn, she began dating a man who loved her feisty empowered side, and the two created a wonderful balance in what they both brought to the connection. Max no longer ran in the other direction when she felt vulnerable or when her new beau wanted to "take care of her." She embraced it, and as a result she was able to transform her previous tendencies, such as running at the first sign of feeling trapped.

In her new dating experience, she brought real clarity and consistency to her motivations, and, as a result she was able to attract toward herself a better, more suited candidate who was more a mirror to the clear and consistent messaging that she was now putting out.

Her relationship-culture started to change and rewire itself based on her new awareness and the more balanced feminine and masculine aspects of her being.

Is There Such a Thing As Just One Soulmate?

I have done a lot of investigating about this topic, and I have concluded that there is not just one soulmate for each human being, but many.

Energetically, we are drawn to, and we tend to be synchronized energetically with, some people who are here to teach us something important about our life's path and challenge us deeply with important lessons about our life's purpose. These people, I feel, are our soulmates. I say this because I see many people working hard at searching for their one soulmate.

I believe that we have many different soulmates and that they are with us sometimes temporarily, sometimes for many lifetimes.

Sometimes when we meet someone who may seem familiar to us; they may in fact be one of our soulmates who has traveled with us for many lifetimes, but who are not necessarily meant to be our partner. Our partner may be our soulmate, but not every soulmate is our partner. To me, it is important to distinguish between soulmate and partner. Sometimes the two might not inhabit the same body!

In his book *Journey of Souls: Case Studies of Life between Lives*, Michael Newton talks about the "life between lives," or "pre-birth planning," whereby you agree to various situations and challenges that you will experience in this life in order to grow and evolve.

Newton says that you even agree, before you reincarnate onto the planet, to make a contract with the people who will be with you in those experiences. The person may be a friend with whom you feel so in tune that you can read their mind, or a love connection who shows you how to truly open your heart and be vulnerable. This person may not necessarily be a love interest whom you are "meant" to be with forever; instead, they may be someone impactful who shares a temporary period of your life with you for a specific lesson — for how long and how intense depends on the situation you find yourself in.

Also consider that a soulmate may be someone you have had repetitive difficulty with and who just won't leave your life because of the circumstances of your connection, such as a member of your family. However, you will learn and grow with this person, and I consider them to be a soulmate as well. You made a contract with this person to be in the same family and to learn with each other some key lessons (positive or negative). The soul connection and synchronicity between these people is very strong and unmistakable.

Chapter 2
Rules for Dating in a Healthy Empowering Way

Over the years, I have developed a set of rules for people to engage in if they are to enjoy wonderful and healthy experiences in their dating lives. Here are some good "rules" to think about as you navigate the dating world.

1. Having Passion Is Attractive to Others
One of the most important aspects of engaging in the dating world is that you need to be in touch with what makes you excited and passionate. Staying true to yourself and to the things and activities that make you interested and interesting is very attractive to others.

The building of your self-esteem depends on your engaging in activities and experiences that make you happy and that you are proud of.

When I am asked the question, "How do I build my self-esteem?" I usually answer that you must engage in an activity you like and set a small goal. Then consistently go about the business of accomplishing this small goal. Then celebrate your win!

Don't set yourself up for failure by setting a goal that is too big. Bite-size goals are the best way to success and to keeping you engaged in a project. This brings an energy of enthusiasm and self-confidence to your being that will be like a beacon that calls out to others who are equally as confident, filled with self-esteem and passionate about their lives as you are. I observe that this kind of pairing makes for the happiest of unions.

Yet I observe that many lose sight of their passions, friends and routines when they meet someone new. This never turns out well.

Case Study: Maintaining Passions
Christy was a happy, passionate Brazilian jiu-jitsu enthusiast. She loved her classes and her exploration of the martial art. Two to three times a week, she was engaged in activities that were related to her training — meditation and dance; the other days of the week, after work, she loved to try new recipes for her new passion of raw/vegan cooking that she had determined was more helpful for her body balance. Her love of nature and walks in parks were what she called "soul-feeding and essential to my well-being."

At a professional networking event, she met Matt, a fun, hip colleague from a different company. The energy between the two of them was electric, and they quickly started to ramp up their dating to almost-daily dinners, frequent sleepovers and every-weekend adventures. They got along like a house on fire!

Christy quickly stopped going to her jiu-jitsu classes in favor of hanging out with Matt and his friends on a patio. They talked endlessly about politics while sharing bar "appies" and beers. Every evening was a sumptuous new restaurant that they explored as Matt was a lover of great burgers and amazing hip restaurants in the downtown core of the city. Christy could not be happier! The weekends were all about film festivals, food festivals and urban-art exploration. Matt was exciting to be around, and Christy was seduced into his world.

When she walked into my office, she told me all about this new wonderful man she was dating, but she could not figure out why she was now suffering from bouts of depression and anxiety. She said she had not had these feelings since her university days. She was totally confused since she and Matt were considering getting more serious.

But something was holding her back, even though she was falling deeply for Matt, and the dating was beginning to dip into more serious relationship land. I asked her what had been going on with her the last time she felt this way. She started to tell me of her university dating experiences. It turned out that Christy was masterful at forgetting all about her own passions as soon as she got into a relationship. She said it eventually happened quite without her noticing. She got seduced into the world of the new relationship. She said she felt almost a "high" when she was infatuated and slowly forgot to tend to her own passions and interests.

Eventually, she woke up and realized that her cup was empty; she felt depleted and sad and began to experience bouts of anxiety. Because this was going on largely unconsciously, she began to tap into her feelings only once they had become too substantial to ignore.

Our work was to teach Christy to be more aware of the feelings that influenced her choices. Her tendency to fall into a "love haze" had dire consequences for her. Staying deeply in touch with the hobbies, people and experiences that make you the person you are is good for your health as well as your relationships and your dating disposition.

Christy had begun to sabotage her connection with Matt because she was starting to resent him and didn't know why. As soon as she got in touch with what was really going on, she chose to tell Matt she would forgo hanging out with him in favor of a jiu-jitsu class, and she let him know she needed to continue to explore her raw/vegan cooking ventures, which he was welcome to join in on. The connection became more balanced as Christy owned her passions and interests and allowed them to take precedence.

Christy needed to reconnect with her own self and her own passions. She started drawing boundaries around what she chose to participate in. Since she was easily dissuaded from her own wants and needs in favor of Matt's, she and I drew up a list of "non-negotiables" regarding what she had to do for herself daily and weekly to create balance.

Her sadness and anxiety lifted as she ate the right food for her body more often and took part in activities that suited her body and style, including more walks in nature, her jiu-jitsu classes, fewer nights out and her raw/vegan eating.

The relationship with Matt was also enriched, and eventually it did evolve past dating and into a more serious relationship.

Matt loved the fact that she had passions, hobbies and non-negotiables. He wanted to learn more about these. They would also spend time apart, which made their time together even richer.

Christy had an unconscious pattern of abandoning her own passions in favor of her partner's, and that became her go-to relationship-culture.

As she deeply explored her subconscious patterns, she was able to rewire her relationship-culture in favor of one that honored herself, while at the same time allowing her to engage profoundly with the person in her life and still maintain boundaries and her own passions.

2. Past Relationship Influences: Learn from the Past

When entering the dating realm, make sure you are firmly planted in the present moment.

The unresolved and unprocessed feelings, traumas and bad-breakup energies of your past relationships are destined to have an impact on you and how you behave in the dating world. For example, you may be subconsciously closed to intimacy even though you swear up and down that you are ready for something new to begin. This subconscious unresolved baggage can be a major block to attracting the suitors you desire.

Case Study: Learning from the Past

MJ wanted to work on her cavernous fear of being cheated on. Years ago, when she was in her early twenties, she had dated someone whom she was deeply in love with. Her love for and devotion to him was so complete and so resolved that she remained in denial of the signs and symptoms that were right in front of her.

Her upbringing also encouraged the pattern of being oblivious and in denial. Her family-culture habitually swept major family secrets under the carpet. Her mother's mother had been committed to a mental institution when MJ was only ten years old, and that had brought about much shame to the family. MJ's mother would constantly tell MJ that it was not okay to talk about anything of that nature.

The tension between her parents was never spoken of either. They would fight loudly at night behind closed doors, and the next morning when MJ asked what had happened, her mother told her that it was just her imagination and nothing was going on. Her mother habitually told MJ that she was too sensitive. So, over the years, MJ slowly trained herself not to be so "sensitive" and to ignore her very clear gut feelings about things.

By the time she got to her dating world, MJ was adept at not noticing what was right in front of her so as not to appear too sensitive. Of course, that coping mechanism, which came straight out of her family of origin, helped her to navigate her family dynamics but compromised her ability to tap into her inner wisdom when it came to her relationship with a boyfriend, who was unfaithful.

She missed some key cues that clearly indicated cheating behavior. For example, she frequently caught him texting someone else and then quickly hiding his phone as she walked into a room.

When he had not shown up for a date they had clearly made, he told elaborate stories about where he had been. He often smelled of another woman's perfume. He had plausible stories for all the inconsistencies. MJ's gut kept screaming that something was wrong, but she kept ignoring it until one day she caught him red-handed at a restaurant in a deep and amorous embrace with another woman.

In hindsight, she regretted having ignored her instincts. She felt such shame over this, but I encouraged her to forgive herself as she had only been falling back on her deep-rooted family-culture as a means to survive. She has since learned to never ignore her gut feelings and has a deep sense of these feelings that she now uses regularly and successfully.

Our gut feelings are often like antennae that can give us a deeper knowing than our much slower brains are able to comprehend.

As I worked with MJ, she told me that she had started dating a lovely fellow, Sal, and that it could not be going better. But she said that she couldn't stop worrying that he might have been cheating on her. I asked her what had led her to believe this. She said she couldn't find any real evidence and that given her history she had been quite diligent in watching for signs of any kind of odd behavior. There were none.

She said they had a deep emotional connectivity between them. She said he was consistent, present, loyal and transparent and that the newest development was that they were about to take it to the next level and introduce their families to each other. Despite all the positive evidence, there was a nagging, gnawing feeling within MJ that was starting to sabotage the relationship with bouts of jealousy, paranoia and overly controlling behavior on her part.

As we dug into the therapy, I notice that MJ was experiencing a kind of post-traumatic stress disorder (PTSD). The trauma of the past cheating relationship, coupled with the deep feelings she had for Sal, had triggered a fear that she might have been missing or ignoring something crucial.

Also as we dug deeper, we found out that the more connected she felt to him, the more she was afraid of losing him. The post-trauma symptoms made her repetitively think about all that she had experienced before with cheating and her family-culture pattern of ignoring everything.

These thoughts made for a cocktail of fears, anxiety and paranoia that these experiences would repeat themselves. She feared profoundly that she would have to dig herself out of the deep emotional gully she had found herself in after the last relationship, when she had been cheated on. Her PTSD symptoms were trying to protect her from an eventual deep disappointment. Yet the evidence did not match reality in this case. When she brought her concerns to him, he only reassured her more by being even more consistently present, affectionate and transparent.

In therapy, I gave MJ the space to express herself about her fears and her experiences. I encouraged her to journal and acknowledge her fears to herself, and while in my office I had her engage her logic when thinking about what was actually going on. I asked her to keep checking her fears out. I asked her, "Do they actually match the reality of the present moment?" In this case, the reality and the evidence did not support her fears.

The process of giving a voice to her fears, writing in a journal and feeling acknowledged, as well as truly looking at the present moment, allowed her nervous system to slowly start to relax. Her obsessive and repetitive thoughts about being cheated on also started to subside substantially. A rewiring of the neural pathways associated with that traumatic past started to occur.

Exercise to Help MJ Get Past Her Patterns of Behavior

We did an exercise that encouraged MJ to start visualizing the part of herself that was filled with fear.

1. I asked her to close her eyes and breathe slowly, and then to zero in on the part of herself that was fearful. After a while of just quietly being with this part of herself, I asked her to dialogue with it. I let her know that this was only a part of her and not all of her. This calmed her down and her breathing began to turn from being a little labored and fast to being slow and easy.

2. I asked her to ask this part of herself what it was *trying* to do for her. Was there a positive purpose for the repetitive fear pattern that kept showing up, even when things seemed to be okay? (In neuro-linguistic programming [NLP], a negative behavior is understood to have a subconscious "positive intention," or positive purpose, in our lives.[3])

3. As MJ made contact with this part of herself, it began to reveal many things to her. She said to me, "The fear shows up when things are going so well because it is trying to protect me from the pain and disappointment I felt when I was totally blindsided by my ex when he cheated on me. It helps me to never again be caught off guard." And so we learned that this part was actually acting as MJ's "protector."

4. I asked her to thank this protector part as it had been doing its job of protecting her but was doing it in a misaligned way that was causing her to feel hypervigilant, on guard and anxious.

5. I asked her to keep dialoguing with this part to see if she could ask it to do its job in a different way that would cause her to feel more at ease.

6. After sitting quietly with her eyes closed for some time, MJ went from being tense to being more relaxed, as if she had come through a bit of a struggle to the other side. She finally emerged and said, "What I am feeling is that this part of me will continue to point out possible areas I need to be aware of, especially if I am in a blind spot. But it will wait for me to investigate and see if

---

[3] Robert Dilts, "The NLP Pattern of the Month: Reframing. The Principle of 'Positive Intention,'" 1995,
http://www.nlpu.com/Patterns/pattern2.htm.

there is any real-life evidence that I need to take care of in an adult and responsible way. It wants to help me to stay out of denial so that I don't follow my family-culture way of dealing with things, such as ignoring the facts. I feel that this aspect encourages me to stay current with what I need emotionally and to keep journaling so that I am in constant touch with my inner voice and my own sense of who I am."

7. I asked MJ to rename her protector part, which was too wrapped up in fear and anxiety, and after some time she called it her "wise-and-aware part," which she described as the part of herself that keeps her in touch with reality in an adult and empowered way and reminds her to love and care for herself by being present, grounded and in touch with the here and now.

8. We were able to transform this misaligned part of her into an aligned version of itself that would help her stay out of past trauma and in present-day reality. This exercise helped to her stop thinking obsessively about her present-day relationship, which she was seeing through the lens of her past dysfunctional relationship. By looking directly at the "monster" that MJ feared so much, she was able to dismantle the power it had over her. She was able to see it for what it actually was and to reframe it so that it became useful to her.[4]

It is also worthwhile to note that sometimes thinking about those negative past experiences can be a positive endeavor, but only if you are able learn from them and, as a result, learn to be the person you would rather be. For example, in a past relationship that ended badly, you might have been overly permissive, saying yes when you did not want to,

---

[4] Ibid.

and then you felt resentful all the time. If you learn appropriately from the past, you will allow the experience to teach you to draw better boundaries in your future relationships. This is the best way for a past relationship to impact you.

3. We Cannot Learn from What We Judge
It is important to understand that when you engage in judgment of self and others, any learning that could have occurred is basically lost.

When you judge yourself, your journey and your patterns, the part of you that can engage in analysis is not as active as the part of you that is condemning and belittling. This causes shame to show up and to do its damage.

When a person feels shame about themselves and their past choices, they are less likely to choose people, places and things that are good for them. They are more likely to engage in self-bullying behavior that usually brings about more pain and more poor choices. It is really a vicious cycle of hell.

Similarly, if you judge others, you are more likely to be coming from a place of righteousness, which leaves little room for real analysis, understanding and compassion. This is not ideal for setting yourself up for learning.

Regarding others, it is most beneficial to allow your mind to try and understand the person you are judging.

You may not want to engage with them ever again, but it is incredibly helpful to find out why they entered your sphere and your life and to understand why you are so triggered by them and their actions.

More Dating Rules of Engagement:

- **Impulsiveness is your enemy.** If you feel like calling or texting just because you are feeling lonely, don't! One call or one text is sufficient, and then let the other person come to you. Trust that they will, and if they don't, then perhaps you are not a match.

When you operate from impulsiveness, your adult self is not engaged. It is important before calling or reaching out in any way that you are mindful that you are not operating from your various child manifestations, such as the hurt child, the rebellious teenager, the deprived and abandoned child, the bored child/teen, the victim, the one in denial, the unaware part, the desperate one and more. The only way to determine this is if you are in touch with your deep self.

An essential component to navigating safely in new relationships is having good and healthy boundaries. The trouble is, most people have a hard time knowing what good boundaries are. Impulsiveness, for example, can indicate poor boundaries. In the case of new relationships and dating, slow is always better if you are to care well for yourself and your soul. Try not to reveal too much of yourself all at once. Move slowly, checking for compatibility and a sense of emotional safety/healthiness first. I think the best way to engage in dating is to make sure you take time each day and each week to tap into your "self" so that you fill you own cup often. That way you're less likely to need others to do that for you. You'll feel less desperate and less in a hurry to have someone else be the main course in your life. I often suggest that those you are dating be the side order, the extra bit versus the main course. The main course works well on its own! If you get a side order or an extra bit, that is a bonus, but it's not essential.

- **Don't get fooled by the "love drug."** When we cuddle and engage in sexual activity, we emit the "nesting hormone" oxytocin, which motivates us to want to nest, sometimes even with the wrong person. It promotes a desire for sexual intimacy before you have been able to establish any emotional intimacy.

If a relationship is what you want to get out of your dating efforts, then I suggest that you not engage in sex for at least a month with the person you are getting to know. I understand that each person has their own sexual moral code, but it is my opinion that the longer you wait for sexual intimacy, the better chance you have of emotional intimacy evolving in a healthy way. Physical intimacy tends to overshadow everything else.

Case Study: The Love Drug

Charlene met a brand new woman, and she told me she was instantly "in love." She wanted to spend all day and night with her. She felt as if she was drugged with this new person's energy, and she couldn't get enough of her. She had worked diligently in therapy to come out and to become comfortable being an openly gay woman. And now with Patti, she felt she needed her daily fix of her and would do whatever it took to keep the feeling alive.

She told me she loved every little thing about Patti and said she didn't want to limit one bit the length of time they were together. Personal time? What personal time? Everything had gone by the wayside in favor of spending time with Patti. The new romance had taken over every part of her life to the point where even her work was suffering.

Charlene had given Patti her house key, and they were practically living together already! After only one month of knowing each other, Charlene had lost all ability to gauge whether or not her choices were good or simply motivated by the "love drug" oxytocin that made her thinking fuzzy and at times illogical.

This almost-obsession with one another at the onset of a new romance is very common. But as time passes, people start to see each other as they really are — each other's flaws. You have your first fight. Even though you both sincerely felt the deepness of the connection at the beginning, the honeymoon has worn off; now the real work begins.

The adventure of entering into a new relationship can be sensational and wondrous. However, it can also be challenging to wade through it in an emotionally safe way unless you are clear about, and aware of, what is actually happening in the relationship.

For Charlene, her trust in Patti was miscalculated. Deep disappointment did occur as she learned that Patti was not nearly as trustworthy as she had assumed. There were clear signs of Patti's carelessness with Charlene's home and possessions. She also discovered that Patti was not as emotionally stable as she thought she was. Patti started having repetitive bouts of rage and anger when things did not go according to plan, and at times she would lash out verbally in an uncontrolled way and then collapse in guilt, and a river of apologies would ensue.

Every episode would leave Charlene dizzy and seriously questioning her choice to have practically moved Patti in without deeper consideration of her own boundaries and emotional safety. She had jumped in without looking, and when she landed, she realized she had fallen on a very hard surface that hurt her badly.

Let's look at that initial seeming addiction to one another. That is the biochemical oxytocin in action. This "nesting hormone" courses through both parties' veins and increases every time they touch or caress, and even more every time they make love. I usually caution my clients against having sex too soon in a relationship due to this pernicious little hormone that can trick the mind into thinking it wants to build a nest with someone, even if the person may not be right for them.

This oxytocin hit can make people ignore clear signs of dysfunction. It can override logic, self-care, healthy boundaries and appropriate romance time management that leads people to abandon themselves, their friends and activities that are outside the relationship's inner sanctum!

A good rule of thumb is to slow the physical intimacy down enough for the emotional intimacy to catch up. We need trust, familiarity, consistency, respect and a proven track record to be authentic and relaxed. That requires time. Rushing into the physical and sensual realms too quickly can result in emotionally rough waters.

Stick your toe in first. Test the water. And then move slowly into it as you become comfortable. That way the hormone love drug will not trick you into falling hopelessly in love with Mr. or Ms. Wrong!

- **Slow it down.** If a serious relationship is your intention as you engage in the dating world, then my philosophy is that for the first three months it is not a good idea to talk to each other every single day. I know that the initial excitement, not to mention the above-mentioned oxytocin, makes people want to see each other all the time, but for a healthy connection, it is important to take time to get to know one another and not become overwhelmed with the other person. Try to keep communication to no more than once or twice a week. Keep your own routines in place. Maintain self-care. Don't rush. Stop often and assess whether what is going on is good. Ask yourself if you are fully grounded in the present moment. Ask yourself if you are focusing too much on the future.

- **Casual Sex.** There is absolutely a place for casual sex in the dating realm, but you need to know yourself very well. Mine your moral code in depth. Boundaries, clarity of communication, emotional self-sufficiency, a desire to explore sexuality in a more expansive way and a very modern outlook on life are a must if one is to healthily engage in casual sex.

Remember that your oxytocin will still be excreted, and it is so important to maintain the above-mentioned cognitive awareness.

I love to recommend the book the *The Ethical Slut: A Guide to Infinite Sexual Possibilities* by Dossie Easton and Catherine A. Liszt. The authors define the term *slut* as "a person of any gender who has the courage to lead life according to the radical proposition that *sex is nice and pleasure is good for you.*"[5]

The authors reclaim the term *slut* from its negative connotation to signify instead a person who happily engages in the enjoyment of sex and the delight of intimacy with others in an ethical and open way rather than with judgment and shame.

---

[5] Dossie Easton and Catherine A. Liszt, *The Ethical Slut: A Guide to Infinite Sexual Possibilities* (San Francisco: Greenery Press, 1997), 4.

The book talks about ways to have multiple concurrent sexual relationships in a fair and honest way and how to deal with issues that may arise, including dealing with boundaries, shame, stigma and moral values.

If casual sex is something you wish to engage in, I recommend that you engage in it in a very conscious way so as to not create any negative after effects such as shame. Also make sure that if you engage in casual sex, you do not devalue yourself or confuse sex with love. I have observed many people engage in casual sex in an unconscious way in that they allow their own boundaries to be broken by giving into what others want instead of checking in with themselves and being clear about what they want. They then lie to themselves that they can handle the casual sex, but in the end, they are actually hurt when the person they just had sex with does not want to deepen the connection. This is a recipe for emotional disaster. Once again, get grounded, mine your feelings, be clear and know yourself before engaging in the emotionally risky territory of casual sex.

- **Give each other space.** Have you ever heard the saying "Familiarity breeds contempt"? This is a valid maxim. The faster you become familiar with one another, the faster you're going to start nitpicking, criticizing and judging each other. So give one another time and space and, of course, draw boundaries. Have a boundary for your personal activities. If you are trying to fill your life with the person you are dating, clearly your life is not full enough with your own sense of self. Ideally, when going into a new relationship, have a strong sense of self. Don't make the other person the center of your life — it never works. Remember, you are the main course in your life; the person you are dating is the side order!

- **Communicating electronically.** In this day and age, dating is certainly not what it used to be. Today people enter the dating pool having to contend with a plethora of electronic ways of connecting — a daunting paradigm for many. But my number-one rule in this realm is this: Do not develop a relationship with a person through texting or messaging. Simply organize the time and date of meeting and then wait to get to know the person live and in person! If you do engage in long conversations through texting or messaging, the inevitable outcome is that you will develop a fantasy as to how this person looks and what this person is like. So often I hear of people finally meeting after weeks of texting/messaging, in which the two people actually developed a bona fide emotional connection only to have it dashed upon meeting in person. Don't waste your time by developing an emotional connection with someone you are only texting with. Spend the time getting to know them in real life!

- **Using texting for flirting once you are dating the person.** There is a place for texting once you are in a relationship. Fun, flirty texts can be a useful preamble to a later date. They can be an exciting and enjoyable buildup of sensual and sexual tension for the couple.

- **Stop emotional dumpster diving.** This is when people lose their self-esteem completely and treat themselves as if they deserve only garbage. They keep going toward people and relationships that are dysfunctional, toxic, even abusive. They settle for anything so as not to be alone. Following are some examples:
    - Having affairs with people who are already in committed relationships
    - Saying yes out of feelings of guilt
    - Lying so as not to disappoint someone else

- Allowing others to manipulate you
- Never taking time for yourself to just be alone
- Being an affirmation junkie; that is, always looking for others' approval and acceptance
- Allowing other people's moods to affect your self-esteem

- **Don't fall in love with someone's potential.** Sometimes a person will come into your life who just doesn't have it together. They have great intentions for their life, but at the moment they are in an unrealized place. It is important, when dating, to accept where the person is at. They may change and become more productive, for example, but if you are thinking of this person as a long-term match, know that there are no guarantees as to how this person will follow through on their goals and claims about what they want to do in their life.

Case Study: Falling in Love with Someone's Potential

Bill and Zack were newly dating. Bill came in for counseling to help get some perspective on his new beau. He said the chemistry was fantastic, and he was quite smitten with Zack. He said Zack was good looking, sexy, polite, generous and a great cook to boot.

Bill was deeply ensconced in his career and always maintained during our therapy sessions that he wanted someone who had a progressive career and a good relationship to money. Bill said they talked endlessly about the future they might have together, which included possibly moving to the countryside and buying a bed and breakfast together and living off their land. The fact that they were on the same page was wonderful for Bill.

However, at that time, Zack was trying to dig himself out of a huge debt that he had incurred through overspending and credit-card mismanagement, and he had been recently laid off from his job as a graphic artist at an ad agency. Bill and Zack were both in their late thirties, and their future goals seemed to be aligned, except that Bill's finances were in great shape, and Zack was in a financial mess with no immediate prospect for resolution.

Prior to meeting Zack, Bill had been working with me on his issues with codependency (about which I go into greater detail in the next chapter). But the main issue

Bill was facing was that he had found himself constantly looking outward to others for approval, and he would compromise his own values and priorities to avoid others' rejection. He came from a family-culture that did not encourage an individual to have a voice — a sense of independence — lest he risk being rejected by his domineering father. To deal with his father, he developed a pattern of abandoning himself in favor of whatever his father or anyone else wanted for him.

Bill had some success at overcoming this by improving his sense of self-value. He made better choices in friendships, and he did a bit of a house cleaning of friends who did not treat him respectfully. Even though he felt the pain and the fear that showed up as he left dysfunctional friendships, he was able to change his patterns on the friendship front. However, getting his "love" relationships onto a healthy track still eluded him. He still became seduced by what he thought was the other person's potential.

Enter Zack, a good-looking man, but not at all in keeping with the goals Bill had set for himself. Zack was in debt and without a job. In this case, Bill thought he could fix

Zack's issues! Zack's spending, from what Bill could tell, was out of control. He treated Bill to lavish dinners and lovely gifts, but then Bill found out that he was living completely on credit and without a plan to fix this.

Clearly, Bill was more in love with Zack's potential than with the reality. Bill's therapy goal when we started was to overcome his blind spots when it came to the men he was dating.

Bill no longer wanted to be in relationships with men who didn't have their lives together, where he would end up feeling compelled to fix them and clean up their messes. And here he was again with Zack, another fixer-upper project that meant he was falling in love with someone's potential again.

Bill worked hard to get clear on what was really going on. He realized that if he was to truly honor his value as a well-put-together man on many fronts, he needed to be open to making space for a similar type of man to come forth. He needed to trust that this would and could happen and that it was okay to be alone until such a time.

This was not easy for Bill, but with courage and with a good community of friendships around him, he decided to take his leave from Zack; this meant he could clear the way to bring into his life a man who had his personal, financial and professional life in order.

- **Tame your inner bully.** Your family-of-origin culture may have been a perfect breeding ground for self-loathing and self-sabotage that then compromised your ability to love and accept yourself as you are. This then promoted an inner-bully voice that plagued your every move, criticizing and minimizing your every choice.

To attain selfhood, achieve your goals and engage in dating/relationships, you need to be gentle with yourself. Often we think that if we can just be disciplined and strict enough with ourselves, we will be more successful. If we don't seem to be getting anywhere, we become impatient and get mad at ourselves, berating, criticizing, judging and yelling at ourselves. Do more! Be more! Go, go, go!

Our intentions are good; we want to be better people and fulfill our potentials, but this kind of self-talk can only cause us to shut down and rebel because it is abusive and devoid of love. It sabotages us and we lose our motivation. Deep inside our beings, we hear the discipline without love and we perceive it as abuse.

The bully in us may be familiar because we have normalized it as a way to motivate ourselves; however, it is rarely effective, at least not for long. In fact, bullying ourselves has the opposite effect. If, for example, you set yourself a New Year's resolution, and then try to achieve it in a militaristic, punishing and rigid manner, you are bound to fail. Why is this? It is because your inner child begins to feel afraid, and so it rebels when you try to move away from your comfort zone. Your inner child says, "I'm afraid of change." "I feel lost." "It feels as though you're punishing me."

Your inner child is screaming to be heard; it wants you to know that it wants to do better, but it wants to be comfortable in this pursuit. For example, if you want to improve your diet, and shock yourself into a new eating regimen that you force on yourself, your system will respond by making you feel profoundly deprived. As a result, you may try to comfort yourself by binge eating, and your entire resolution goes down the drain.

To create a new pattern of behavior, you need to transform the bully voice within you into a supportive coach voice that eases you gently into the desired change. In reality, the bully is *trying* to make you a better you, but in a misdirected way. To transform your inner bully, you need to speak to it as you would to a child who is frightened and throwing a tantrum. If you yell at the bully, it will simply yell back more loudly. To make a connection, you need to speak gently to it.

I invite you to practice a visualization to help you transform your inner bully. See appendix B, "Visualization to Transform Your Inner Bully into a Supportive Coach." This exercise, when practiced often, can help you to rewire your neural pathways away from this pattern.

The more open you are, the more information you will gather, and the more likely you will be able to neutralize and, ultimately, transform your destructive inner bully.

If you listen carefully, the bully will tell you that it is *trying* to make you a better person. It is *trying* to protect you from failure and disappointment. It is *trying* to encourage you to be the best you can be. However, as you know, it is failing miserably at this task because of its abusive tone.

It is important that you understand that this is a process of befriending your darker side; that is, integrating it into your whole being so that it knows that you are finally listening carefully to its underlying positive message, and that it will not have to yell as loudly at you to be heard. This type of inner dialogue is the way to transform the bully within yourself.

- **Jealousy.** If jealousy is a problem, then it is so important to understand its underlying causes, especially if there is no cause for jealousy. Unfounded jealousy has its roots in issues of lack of a sense of self-value. On analysis, we find that a person who engages in jealousy is not taking good care of their "self." They are falling down on good self-care routines; they do not value themselves and often engage in a lot of self-deprecating talk. Pay attention to your own needs and self-care routine. Grounding and connection to self to lessen insecurities are paramount.

  If unfounded jealousy is something you struggle with, work on making sure that your self-care routine is active. How are you feeling in your body? How are you feeling regarding your inner running commentary? Are you taking your vitamins? Are you eating well? Are you exercising? Are you doing the things that you love to do? Are you tending to your own passions? Are you journaling? Is your relationship with yourself a good one? Make sure that the various areas of your life are being nurtured so that you feel full and loving toward yourself. All of this is so important to maintain a solid self-esteem and to lessen the jealousy gremlins, which, if left unmanaged, are sure to ruin your relationships.

- **Make a list!** A fun but effective tool I use often in my office with clients who are in the dating world and are having trouble meeting compatible people is the making of a long and detailed list. I ask clients to close their eyes and focus on how they would like to *feel* once they are in a relationship with the ideal person. This is not about the other person's hair color and height; it is more about personality and character traits that make them feel the way they want to feel when they are with that person. I encourage clients to be less concerned about *how* they will meet the right person. Instead, I ask them to be clear about *what* they wish to *feel* with the right person. Here are examples of what to add to your list:

- We have wonderful chemistry together.
- This person loves to make me laugh.
- I feel relaxed and at ease with this person.
- We are compatible in our tastes and likes.
- We are sexually attracted to each other.
- This person's financial house is in order.
- This person has a good relationship with his/her family.
- This person has resolved his/her childhood issues or is working on them.
- We match at our cores.
- This person challenges me.
- This person accepts me.
- I accept this person.
- I have deep trust in this person.
- This person is loyal and true to me.
- This person has my back.
- This person is my greatest cheerleader.
- This person safeguards my reputation.
- I respect this person and his/her values.

The energetic principle that states, "What we focus on expands" is an important principle to work with. The more you clearly focus on what you would like to draw toward yourself, the better.

Visualizing in great detail is an act of sending a clear message out to the Universe as to what you would like to attract toward yourself. The clearer you are, the more laser beam–like your intentions will be, and the more you are likely to bring that very person toward you.

But the more confused you are, the more the energy you are putting out is dispersed and watered down, and you will be less likely to draw toward yourself the person who matches you. Once you have your list, I encourage you to look at it daily and visualize what it would be like to have that person in your life. Work on trusting all will work out well.

Try not to dilute your intentions with negative thinking. Say the following affirmations every time you complete the visualizing process:

- Everything is working out better than I expect.
- This or something better is now manifesting for me.
- I trust in the timing and in the process of life.

I have seen this list-making exercise work amazingly well. But don't take my word for it, I invite you to try this on for yourself and test it out. But make sure the list you create is not simply about looks. You want to create a list that brings on much deeper aspects than simply physical appearance.

It also bears saying that it is important to get your own house in order. If you are looking to attract someone toward yourself who has dealt with their childhood issues, then please make sure you are working on yours as well.

If you want to draw in someone who has a good relationship with money, then please make sure you have that aspect of your life in order too.

And, if you want someone who is emotionally stable, make sure you have worked on your emotions to create stability as well.

In short, whatever you are looking for in another person, you need to have it living in you as well, or at least be consciously working on it.

Part II

Spotting Relationship Dysfunction From the Start

"Overcoming codependency depends on your making yourself a priority and focusing on you and your issues and problems versus others'. You need to declare to yourself that you are valuable and you have a right to your needs, your voice, and your wants. You may not get those needs met by the other person, but first and foremost it is important that you start to focus on yourself — realize that you matter and that you have needs."
- Victoria Loient-Faibish

Chapter 3
Codependency

Knowledge is power! It is important when dating and entering a relationship to be armed with knowledge about different personality types so you feel more empowered as you navigate this territory.

As you go about the business of *not* repeating old patterns from your family-culture, you begin the process of rewiring your beliefs and patterns of behavior. But change requires profound awareness and a willingness to do something different. This is the process of creating a healthy relationship-culture!

In this chapter I discuss the relationship dysfunction of codependency so that you can spot it if you come across it in yourself and in your relationships. In the next two chapters I examine the narcissistic personality and the almighty and deceptive Commitment Phobia.

Codependency Chaos

Codependency is a pattern of behavior that evolves out of the family-of-origin and family-culture experience. Essentially, it is a symptom, a survival pattern that a person develops over time through what they observed and experienced early in life. It is prevalent and normalized in society to the point that it can be hard to spot. But left unchecked, it can do real damage and make a relationship dysfunctional. Let's face it, society says it's better to give than to receive, so we have a whole system — media, society and religious cultures that say it's better to give than to receive. It is beautiful to give. I love being generous. But there has to be a balance — a give and take. It is impossible to sustain constant depletion of your vessel — your being. If you give, give, give, you will have nothing left and you will be giving from an empty vessel. When this happens, not only are you susceptible to disease because you are so depleted, but also the part of you that has needs expresses itself in rogue ways.

Codependent people who have been squashed can become the people who have affairs. This is the rogue behavior that they might engage in to get their needs met in the only way they think they can. We have all heard stories in the media where a self-professed do-gooder religious leader claims to live a profoundly selfless life, and then later we discover they are expressing themselves in rogue ways through extramarital affairs, lies, cheating and living double lives. You can see how much pain, shame and self-loathing they go through when the mask finally falls and they are sadly exposed. As I have observed this, my only hope for them has been that their profound discomfort leads to a crash or a breakdown, and then, if they're lucky, they may end up in a therapist's office to dig themselves out of the mess they have created so that they can finally live a truly authentic and balanced life.

When I work with codependent people, I find it is best to treat their codependency like an addiction. Not so much an addiction to a substance, but to people and patterns of behavior, within and outside relationships. I define addiction as "engaging in a pattern that you know is harmful to yourself or another but that you are unable to stop doing. It is a compulsion to behave in a certain way to avoid certain painful feelings or states of being." The addiction is the symptom of the pain. In this case, we are speaking of the addiction of codependency, which is actually a symptom of a deeper core issue that needs to be dealt with before it becomes destructive.

To make matters worse, codependency seems to be an acceptable behavior in society and in the media, where a plethora of codependent relationships get billed as healthy and functional. Relationships in soap operas, movies and reality TV seem to readily embody the "I-can't-live-without-you" battle cry or the "I-need-to-be-needed" compulsive feeling or the "I-need-to-find-a-solution-to-the-problem-I-observe-in-you" obsession, and they set that up as a model people ought to strive for in relationships in real life. This gets confused with passion or real love.

So often I have seen folks putting a good relationship on the chopping block because there is not enough drama and neediness or jealousy. They say they feel bored in their relationship, and they'll say, "I want a soulmate," which they confuse with neediness, drama, control, overenmeshment, jealousy and emotional dependency. They compare what they learned in their family-culture or what they see in the mainstream media with their own lives and think that is what is healthy for a long-term passionate relationship. Instead, they actually crave the familiar — a recipe for dysfunction, trauma and unhappiness.

Another good description of codependency is "when a person's self-esteem rises and falls based on the other person's mood, tone or experience." But it is actually much more than that. The person is overly involved in the other person's needs, wants, problems and issues. In reality, some of the nicest people in the world are codependent, and if not watched, all relationships have the potential to become codependent. Codependency takes healthy emotions and corrupts them. For example, empathy is a positive emotion, but in codependency the empathy rises to a level where there is no division between the two people. Generosity is also a beautiful emotion, but in codependency it turns into control and overenmeshment. In addition, the codependent person often feels excessively guilty for having any need that may create discomfort in the other person, even if the need is healthy and necessary for their emotional well-being. The obsession of not hurting the other person is taken to levels of deep dysfunction. The codependent person needs to take care of or fix the other person. Their own needs are muted and buried. These are nice people, but, unfortunately, the codependent person's needs and well-being are totally and constantly second to the other person's needs. They find value only when they are preoccupied with the other person's life, problems, issues and difficulties. *They are most comfortable and motivated by feeling needed and depended on.* That is what is most familiar to them, and their self-esteem goes up at the very thought of this.

The problem that many codependents run into is that their self-esteem is dependent on other people appreciating them, depending on them, admiring them and liking them. This is a precarious place on which to put one's self-esteem since there can be absolutely no control over how other people think or feel. And since there is a 50-50 chance that someone will admire or like you when you do something for them, there is a great risk that your self-esteem will take a real nosedive if the people you are helping do not appreciate things that you do for them.

When I work with a codependent person who inevitably is having relationship trouble, I ask about their needs, wants, desires and inner thoughts. Upon asking this question, I have witnessed a combination of emotional paralysis, sadness, anger and even a full anxiety attack occur at the very prospect of having to define what their needs and wants are. Codependency is deeply ingrained in a person's very matrix. They are trained from a young age to abandon their own needs and wants in favor of the other person's. The family of origin has deep in its culture a way of being that does not allow the individual to feel their inner feelings and act on them. The family-culture promotes the concept that the group is more important than the individual.

Another reason I see codependency as an addiction is that people experience almost a high when they are fixing someone else's life. They are preoccupied with helping someone else, but they are completely out of touch with themselves. They get a sense of self-value since the act of taking care of someone else brings on a feeling of immense empathy and compassion.

Subconsciously, and at times quite consciously, they will do anything to avoid dealing with their own wants and needs. It's almost painful to them. It's too much pressure, so solving another person's problems is an appealing, societally vetted escapist activity. The codependent person needs another person with problems and issues to fix. However, serving, or helping, the other person inevitably leads to the other person's "underfunctioning." It's like a magnet; the underfunctioner looks for the "overfunctioner," and the overfunctioner looks to keep the underfunctioner in an underfunctioning place. It's a match made in hell because, inevitably, the overfunctioner soon becomes resentful of the underfunctioner. The codependent starts to feel angry that the other person is so dependent, yet they have set up that environment by constantly fixing the other person. That dynamic has become an unharmonious dance that eats away at the health of the relationship. It is a tough pattern to break because the codependent has gotten all of their identity from the other person.

Where does this all start? Usually codependency begins when a person is very young — under seven, although I have seen a person become codependent later in life. But for the sake of understanding how this pattern of behavior can evolve, let's look at how it might begin in childhood. Possibly the child senses that the parent is not tending to their needs in the way they need, either because the parent is too busy, there's too much going on, there's emotional and financial chaos, the parent has an addiction or the parent is simply inept. Let me be clear that this is not about parent-blaming. Parenting is one of the hardest jobs for which there is no training. But it is important to understand the impact of certain childhood events that can impact a person to engage later in life in patterns of behavior that are less than healthy, and which, in turn, create dysfunctional adult relationships. Also, this may not be just about the parents but about the entire family-culture that has embodied a collection of patterns and habits multigenerationally.

If the child senses that they constantly and consistently cannot get their needs met, the child may become apathetic, thinking, "Why bother even having needs? Every time I have a need, my parent either ignores me, mocks me, shuts me down, stops me from feeling or doesn't give me what I need," so they stop having the needs. Or the child can become "the hard-working baby." Hard-working babies realize they have to do it all for themselves. They have to work hard to get any love or approval, and often these children may learn to talk and walk relatively early because they subconsciously sense it is better to not bother the parent. These children feel nervous, even anxious, when they have a need or have to call upon the parent. Later in life, they will be drawn to these kinds of dynamics in their relationships — dynamics that they have normalized for themselves. As adults, the pattern turns into the disease-to-please — constantly apologizing for themselves, not knowing what their needs are, constantly looking to others for approval and repeatedly overfocusing on the other person's problems over their own; that is, overfunctioning. On the other hand, the pattern may turn into the need to have control at all cost, overenmeshment and the need to fix. In short, codependency thus becomes their relationship-culture.

Case Study: Codependency

Olga came from a deeply loving family. But as the youngest child and only girl, she was told from the time she could walk that her purpose was to "help" her two brothers and her parents.

This later translated into her doing most if not all the chores. She had to rush home after school to cook for the boys because Mom and Dad were working at the demanding family business. She was not allowed to do any after-school activities since the chores took priority.

Her brothers played football and did track-and-field after school, and Olga needed to make sure they had good meals to come home to.

For her whole young life, it was her duty to make sure her brothers were fed, clean, happy and taken care of. Her desire to join the after-school theater group or the choir were looked down on since her duties at home were considered a priority she had to respect.

As she got older, she balked a little and tried to convince her parents that the boys could look after themselves, but the whole family did not allow this to transpire. They said it was selfish of her to think of herself.

The boys needed her. The family counted on her. She was valued for her service, and so, over time, she got used to this. She found her identity became wrapped up in playing the role of the caretaker of the family.

When Olga finally got to the age where she began dating, she had no idea how to conduct herself in a modern relationship where two people have equal rights to occupy space. Throughout her dating life she lived the repetitive pattern of caretaking and forgetting herself.

When she eventually became serious with a man, this pattern intensified as she embarked on a journey of replicating her family-culture dynamics in her adult relationship, and she tended only to his needs and forgot her own. This became her relationship-culture. Even though she had set up the pattern, she found herself deeply resentful over time but could not change her pattern. She was a full-blown codependent, and even though she knew intellectually that her repetitive actions were not healthy and balanced, she did not know how to stop.

In fact, even though her partner encouraged her point-blank to "self-care" and be less involved with taking care of him because he felt she was controlling, she was not able to stop and even felt resentful when he asked this of her. However, whenever she did try to stop, she felt out of sorts. She actually felt empty and depressed when she was not involved in caring for him and his life.

It was clearly Olga's relationship-culture that eventually destroyed her relationship. She was unable to stop her overenmeshment in her boyfriend's life, and he felt smothered and eventually decided to leave the relationship.

Olga had to do some very deep work to break this pattern of behavior and rewire the neural pathways associated therein. The journey ultimately was about Olga's looking at herself and seeing how she could deposit all of those caring instincts and patterns into herself first so that she could know herself and feel her feelings as opposed to completely ignoring herself and overfocusing on others. She started to attend a Co-Dependents Anonymous (CoDA) group in addition to the therapy she was doing with me. The climb out of the codependent trap is not easy, but it is doable, and Olga was able to slowly go through the profound discomfort of creating a new relationship-culture through awareness and courage.

Patterns and Characteristics of Codependence

Following is a list of patterns and characteristics of codependence to help you spot it. As you go on the journey to rewire your relationship-culture, the more you know about this, the better. Co-Dependents Anonymous lists some patterns and characteristics of codependency that may assist you in determining if you are, in fact, a codependent type of person or if you are in a codependent relationship.[6]

Ask yourself if any of the following apply to you:
Denial Patterns
- I have difficulty identifying what I am feeling.
- I minimize, alter, or deny how I truly feel.
- I perceive myself as completely unselfish and dedicated to the well-being of others.
- I lack empathy for the feelings and needs of others.
- I label others with my negative traits.
- I can take care of myself without any help from others.

---

[6] *The Patterns and Characteristics of Codependency* is reprinted here with the permission of Co-Dependents Anonymous, Inc.

- I mask my pain in various ways such as anger, humor, or isolation.
- I express negativity or aggression in indirect and passive ways.
- I do not recognize the unavailability of those people to whom I am attracted.

Low Self-Esteem Patterns
- I have difficulty making decisions.
- I judge what I think, say, or do harshly, as never good enough.
- I am embarrassed to receive recognition, praise, or gifts.
- I value others' approval of my thinking, feelings, and behavior over my own.
- I do not perceive myself as a lovable or worthwhile person.
- I constantly seek recognition that I think I deserve.
- I have difficulty admitting that I made a mistake.
- I need to appear to be right in the eyes of others and will even lie to look good.
- I am unable to ask others to meet my needs or desires.
- I perceive myself as superior to others.
- I look to others to provide my sense of safety.
- I have difficulty getting started, meeting deadlines, and completing projects.
- I have trouble setting healthy priorities.

Compliance Patterns
- I am extremely loyal, remaining in harmful situations too long.
- I compromise my own values and integrity to avoid rejection or anger.
- I put aside my own interests in order to do what others want.

- I am hypervigilant regarding the feelings of others and take on those feelings.
- I am afraid to express my beliefs, opinions, and feelings when they differ from those of others.
- I accept sexual attention when I want love.
- I make decisions without regard to the consequences.
- I give up my truth to gain the approval of others or to avoid change.

Control Patterns
- I believe most people are incapable of taking care of themselves.
- I attempt to convince others what to think, do, or feel.
- I freely offer advice and direction to others without being asked.
- I become resentful when others decline my help or reject my advice.
- I lavish gifts and favors on those I want to influence.
- I use sexual attention to gain approval and acceptance.
- I have to be needed in order to have a relationship with others.
- I demand that my needs be met by others.
- I use charm and charisma to convince others of my capacity to be caring and compassionate.
- I use blame and shame to emotionally exploit others.
- I refuse to cooperate, compromise, or negotiate.
- I adopt an attitude of indifference, helplessness, authority, or rage to manipulate outcomes.
- I use terms of recovery in an attempt to control the behavior of others.
- I pretend to agree with others to get what I want.

Avoidance Patterns
- I act in ways that invite others to reject, shame, or express anger toward me.

- I judge harshly what others think, say, or do.
- I avoid emotional, physical, or sexual intimacy as a means of maintaining distance.
- I allow my addictions to people, places, and things to distract me from achieving intimacy in relationships.
- I use indirect and evasive communication to avoid conflict or confrontation.
- I diminish my capacity to have healthy relationships by declining to use all the tools of recovery.
- I suppress my feelings or needs to avoid feeling vulnerable.
- I pull people toward me, but when they get close, I push them away.
- I refuse to give up my self-will to avoid surrendering to a power that is greater than myself.
- I believe displays of emotion are a sign of weakness.
- I withhold expressions of appreciation.

I want to highlight a few of the above patterns. Codependent people often perceive themselves as completely unselfish and dedicated to the well-being of others. This is the Mother Theresa codependent person.

Seemingly perfectly unselfish, but, my goodness, inside there is a seething resentment growing and building like lava that will explode out of a volcano.

Codependent people are constantly valuing others' approval over their own thinking, feelings and behavior.

Seeking others' opinions and guidance is a good endeavor; however, with codependency the mind is so overly focused on what other people's opinions are that the person is deprived of building the very important muscle of self-exploration and a strong inner voice.

People sense the pressure and the lack of relaxation that infuses the air of codependency. The destruction is akin to a parasite taking hold of the host and eventually taking over and destroying it.

And then there are the control patterns. This is interesting because it can seem that the pattern of control is not the domain of the ever-benevolent codependent person.

However, codependent people constantly have their tentacles out, feeling everyone in the room, trying to figure out what each person is feeling and thinking.

They are looking to anticipate whatever they think needs anticipating so as not to be blindsided. They need to feel that they have a handle on or control over any given situation. Most if not all spontaneity goes out the window. The joy of being in the moment is lost.

Codependent people believe most other people are incapable of taking care of themselves, and they, in their infinite wisdom and generosity, know what is best for the other person. I see this as control through generosity, which can be deceptive and eventually destructive to a relationship since the generosity always has an agenda attached to it.

The codependent person's cocktail of overenmeshment, overcontrol, overcompassion and overgenerosity becomes the poison that eventually destroys any freedom or any healthiness for both parties involved.

People often ask me, "Aren't we all codependent?" Yes, it is true. It is common, but that still does not make it healthy.

And, sadly, it is such an insidious and capricious pattern that it goes largely unnoticed or is disguised as a very generous person.

But it always becomes problematic and laden with guilt, resentment and volatility.

Left untreated, it only increases and does more damage.

Keys to Healing Codependency:

The first and most important step in stopping codependency in yourself is awareness that you engage in the pattern.

Also, if you are in a relationship with a codependent person, chances are you are one as well. The relationship has taken on the pattern of codependency in most, if not all, of its dealings.

As I mentioned earlier, I feel that the way out is to treat the condition as an addiction. And, as such, it will not be easy to unravel. There are amazing free 12-step groups that you can attend, online and in person, with an organization called Co-Dependency Anonymous.

Engaging in therapy would also be very helpful in moving away from this stubborn and insidious pattern. You cannot overcome this alone. The more support you get the better.

Overcoming codependency depends on your making yourself a priority and focusing on you and your issues and problems versus others'. You need to declare to yourself that you are valuable and you have a right to your needs, your voice, and your wants. You may not get those needs met by the other person, but first and foremost it is important that you start to focus on yourself — realize that you matter and that you have needs.

Change requires three main elements: (1) *Awareness* to see with clarity what is truly going on, (2) *Willingness* to do whatever it takes to move into a shift and (3) *Courage* to face this sometimes immensely challenging process toward authenticity.

When I work with clients who present with codependency patterns, I encourage them to work on the following:

- Start to acknowledge and take care of your own needs so healing from codependency can begin to happen.

- Read all of Melody Beattie's books, including *Codependent No More: How to Stop Controlling Others and Start Caring for Yourself.*

- Immediately find a hobby to engage in and develop a routine to stick to.

- Stop being motivated by wanting to have others like you or depend on you.

- Remember that *only you can build your self-esteem.* For example, by setting a small goal, accomplishing it and feeling good about yourself. Bit by bit your self-esteem will become more solid.

- Join a 12-step group so you can share with people with similar problems. Such groups include Adult Children of Alcoholics/Dysfunctional Families (ACA) and Co-Dependents Anonymous (CoDA).

- Work consistently to heal any childhood traumas through private therapy, group therapy, meditation and/or self-care.

- Write down your feelings. Keeping a journal is a great way to vent and express yourself, and it will help you get through the scary initial phases of change.

- Create new neural pathways: It takes, on average, twenty-one days to create a new habit, and within that time you will be creating new neural pathways that correspond with the new behavior. Practice, practice, practice the new behavior.

- Keep the 80/20 rule: You move in the new direction 80% of the time, and you can allow yourself to slide back into old ways the other 20% of the time. This is a gentler way to create change that will not feel like self-bullying, but instead like a supportive coach guiding you into a new way of being.

- Feel the pain, the discomfort, the fear, but take on the new behavior anyway. A person who is overcoming such an ingrained pattern as codependency will feel discomfort upon making the changes, but that is part of the process.

- Work diligently at *not* jumping back into the other person's life as soon as you feel discomfort in your own life.

- Know that your relationships will shift once you start to recover from this "addiction." (The people in your life will find it strange, even difficult, to deal with the new "you" that you are offering; however, in time a new normal will ensue.)

- Be mindful: Know that recovering from codependency is not a one-shot deal. I invite you to work mindfully on changing your patterns of behavior.

Chapter 4
Narcissism

Personality Confidential

There are many personality disorders that contribute to relationship dysfunction, but the one I would like to focus in on in this chapter is the "narcissistic personality." This is supremely important to spot when engaged in the dating and relationship realms.

One of my favorite definitions of a personality disorder states: "A personality disorder is an enduring pattern of inner experience and behavior that deviates from the norm of the individual's culture.

The pattern is seen in two or more of the following areas: cognition; affect; interpersonal functioning; or impulse control. The enduring pattern is inflexible and pervasive across a broad range of personal and social situations. It typically leads to significant distress or impairment in social, work or other areas of functioning. The pattern is stable and of long duration, and its onset can be traced back to early adulthood or adolescence."[7]

In reality, when dealing with a personality disorder, there is no fixing or changing the person. The person's partner cannot love them into wellness, health and happiness. Awareness of the symptoms is important so you can make good decisions for yourself when you encounter them in your dating and relationship travels.

---

[7] Psych Central, "Narcissistic Personality Disorder Symptoms," 2014, http://psychcentral.com/disorders/narcissistic-personality-disorder-symptoms.

Narcissism
The world is abuzz with demonstrations of narcissism.

We see narcissism more than ever in the media nowadays, with all the selfies and glorification of larger-than-life personalities. There seems to be a love-hate relationship with this trait, which ranges from annoying to pathological.

We all have narcissistic tendencies. In fact, as babies we're all about "Me!" Feed me, love me, talk to me, see me. This is part of our biological survival instinct.

The narcissism of babies often becomes socialized out of us through the learning of empathy for others when our parents are loving, non-narcissistic and non-violent and the child isn't traumatized.

What turns a baby's narcissism into a personality disorder later in life is not clear. The reality is that researchers do not have a definitive cause for narcissism.

It may have biopsychosocial causes, in which the biological, genetic, social and psychological factors all come together, including the innate temperament of the person to form a patterning in response to a stress. There is evidence that shows that children of narcissistic parents tend to be more at risk for developing the personality disorder.[8]

We tend to repeat and mirror our parental issues in a bid to resolve them, fix them, survive them and understand them in some way. Children who have had to cope with a narcissistic, often abusive parent have had to become

---

[8] John Thomas Steinbeck, "The Narcissistic Parent," January 28, 2011, http://www.brainwashingchildren.com/the-narcissistic-parent.

narcissistic themselves in order to survive the berating, criticism, shaming, mocking, selfishness, inconsideration and bullying.

Or they may have been the first-born male child in a family that prized and aggrandized the male gender above all, leading them to become full of themselves to the point of narcissism.

In reality, any gender can be aggrandized by their parents in an exaggerated way. It is important to be able to spot this early in a relationship, lest you become embroiled and traumatized by such a personality in your partner.

The Mayo Clinic defines *narcissistic personality disorder* as "a mental disorder in which people have an inflated sense of their own importance, a deep need for admiration and a lack of empathy for others. But behind this mask of ultraconfidence lies a fragile self-esteem that's vulnerable to the slightest criticism."[9]

The *Diagnostic and Statistical Manual of Mental Disorders*, fifth edition (DSM-5) lists the following features included in the criteria for narcissistic personality disorder:[10]

- Having an exaggerated sense of self-importance
- Expecting to be recognized as superior even without achievements that warrant it
- Exaggerating your achievements and talents

---

[9] Mayo Clinic, "Narcissistic Personality Disorder: Definition," 2015, http://www.mayoclinic.org/diseases-conditions/narcissistic-personality-disorder/basics/definition/con-20025568.
[10] Mayo Clinic, "Narcissistic Personality Disorder: Symptoms," 2015, http://www.mayoclinic.org/diseases-conditions/narcissistic-personality-disorder/basics/symptoms/con-20025568.

- Being preoccupied with fantasies about success, power, brilliance, beauty or the perfect mate
- Believing that you are superior and can only be understood by or associate with equally special people
- Requiring constant praise and admiration
- Having a sense of entitlement
- Expecting special favors and unquestioning compliance with your expectations
- Taking advantage of others to get what you want
- Having an inability or unwillingness to recognize the needs and feelings of others
- Being envious of others and believing others envy you
- Behaving in an arrogant or haughty manner

I would add the following to that list:
- Expressing disdain for those you feel are inferior
- Being easily hurt and rejected
- Having a fragile sense of self-esteem
- Appearing tough-minded or unemotional
- Being jealous of others and believing others are jealous of you
- Having trouble keeping healthy relationships
- Setting unrealistic goals

Narcissists often feel that they are the victim of perceived rejection or criticism that they are extremely sensitive to.

They often do not seek therapy as that doesn't fit the image they have of themselves that they are too special for that.

Sometimes they do give in and go to therapy because they are depressed due to their perceived rejection by the people whom they have mistreated.

However, the therapy is rarely successful.

Many aspects of a person with narcissistic personality disorder may appear to be confident, but don't be fooled. A person with this disorder goes overboard in their sense of self-confidence, thinking that they should be put on a pedestal and that they have much more value than anyone else.

Narcissists are affirmation junkies. They need you to constantly tell them they are wonderful, but they do not offer the same to others. They rarely care about what you're feeling, but they have a bottomless pit in their need for praise that you cannot fix through endless praise.

The emotions of everyone in the room come second to the narcissist's emotions. If you are in a relationship with a narcissist, you will feel that you are always in the wrong and you are the one who needs to apologize.

In addition, your success will be a major problem for the narcissist, who will seek to bring you down in some way.

Initially, narcissists can be seductive and charming, but once they conquer you, the experience will change. They will often go into victim mode and manipulate a person into feeling guilty. This can be traumatizing for the people who are in a relationship with them. And it will take time to recover after this kind of a relationship.

The arrogance of the narcissist is a cover-up for an insecure individual who has no real desire to work on their insecurities in a real way.

If you find yourself in a relationship with a narcissist who constantly makes you feel bad for having feelings or successes, makes you feel guilty for having needs and wants and denigrates you and other people, then I invite you to consider this a "run, don't walk" situation!

Also, please do not think that they will change. They don't change! They're not interested in therapy. Don't bring them in because therapy is not for a narcissist.

The only way you know they're not a narcissist is if they want therapy and want to work on it. Narcissists who have ended up in my office with their partner are not interested in work; they are interested only in criticizing their partner and the therapist.

They say to themselves and whomever will listen, "I am not interested in therapy. *You* are the one with the problem. I don't have a problem. How dare you even think I have a problem!" That's the battle cry of the narcissist.

In summary, the key to spotting a narcissistic personality is that they are charming and seductive as they gain your favor and trust, and then they turn around and constantly make you feel bad about yourself for having needs, wants, thoughts and successes.

The narcissist has a fragile sense of self-esteem, which is why they go into victim mode when they're called on about their behavior, so you can never make any headway if you call them on it.

Don't confuse this with something that will go away. It doesn't. My heart goes out to anyone in a relationship with a narcissist.

Chapter 5
Commitment Phobia

One of my readers came to me with the following scenario and some questions: "I've been in many wrong relationships and tried to break my cycle of going to the same type of partner. I have been single for about two years now. My last relationship ended due to physical assault. I enjoy being single, but I would like to find my special someone to grow old with. Every time I find myself getting close in a relationship, I panic. I start getting antsy because now I have to compromise with a partner and share. Then I start making excuses for why it would never work, or I pull back, or I find faults in them. Is this commitment phobia? I always thought I was too picky. How picky can one be?"

The simple answer is yes, an aspect of commitment phobia is being overly fault-finding in the other person. Many people with commitment phobia engage in this type of overpickiness as a defense mechanism that doesn't allow them to be okay with the person they are in a relationship with. As soon as the relationship gets a little more comfortable and familiar, they get antsy, which is an anxiety response, possibly triggered by some sort of trauma.

Many of the origins of commitment phobia, as with narcissism, come from a difficult family of origin or a traumatic relationship history. In both cases, trauma, addictions, betrayal, violence, yelling and screaming, criticizing or emotional abandonment may result in a person asking themselves, "Why would I trust in love when love has always been painful? Or in relationships if they've always been difficult? Uncomfortable? Traumatic?"

Commitment-phobes develop an intricate process of denying; they shut themselves down as soon as a relationship becomes a little more intertwined or as intimate as a family relationship. In their minds and bodies, anything that seems even remotely like a family relationship that feels comfortable or intimate brings on a feeling of panic. So their system screams, "I'm outta here!"

Much like the narcissist, a commitment-phobe can also be seductive initially. That's why I tell people to watch out for this dysfunction as it can engulf them. They show up as charming and seductive, and they are so amazing to be around — at first. The energy around this type of individual is all about bringing you into their lair! They may not be doing this on purpose, but this is what occurs. Once you are in there, an instant push-pull begins. "I want you, I want you. Oh, sorry, I don't want you! It's all too much. I'm out." And then, "I want you again." And this repetitive dance continues down a rabbit hole of hell! They are also into the thrill of the hunt, where as soon as they "get" the person, that's it! It's game over as soon as they win. Once they get what they want, they lose interest.

Also, commitment-phobes tend to lie and fabricate — not all of them, but there's a lot of story-making and surprise disappearing acts with commitment-phobic people. A person in a relationship with a commitment-phobe will frequently be the recipient of elaborate stories that explain their periodic disappearing acts. There's a panic that sets in with the commitment-phobe, so they don't feel as though they can come clean. They feel their lying somehow allows them to get away with their actions without the consequence of hurting anyone. They are also subconsciously filled with shame and guilt, so they have to find a story to cover up for the sometimes seemingly insane behavior.

Case Studies: Commitment Phobia

I have two interesting case studies on commitment phobia. The first is a woman, Joss, who was in a relationship with a commitment-phobe, and the second was a male, Marty, who was a commitment-phobe himself.

Joss

Joss was an incredibly intelligent and beautiful woman who was profoundly codependent. She was the kind of person who was constantly solving and fixing the other person's problems. So, of course, she became easy prey for the commitment-phobe who entered her life.

She was ready to serve, do, fix, accommodate and help, and he said, "Excellent!" He seduced her and brought her into his lair. Flowers, trips, months of fun, travel, passion, even deep love came into the mix.

They said their "I love you's" often. They made plans, they met each other's families.

Then — he disappeared. She didn't know where he was for weeks on end. He never called. He never wrote.

All of a sudden he showed up one day with flowers.

"Where the heck have you been?" she asked.

"Oh don't ruin this day with all your questions," he answered. "Aren't we having a beautiful moment here? Aren't these flowers amazing? I picked and arranged them myself! You aren't acknowledging the effort I made for you! Can't you just enjoy this?"

It was a crazy-making experience for her. She wasn't ever able to relax. Her own codependency made her think,

"Maybe I'm the one who is in the wrong. Maybe I can fix this. Maybe he needs more compassion." She put his needs ahead of her own and always played the therapist-fixer. This back and forth went on for three years.

One day he presented her with a massive ring, and so they were engaged. She was deliriously happy. They set a date. She got caught up in the whole whirlwind of the wedding planning. They planned the party together, and a week before the wedding, her niggling doubts started to scream relentlessly at her, making her decide that she needed to get some answers from him about his frequent absences.

Her realization that they were, in fact, going to be married had begun to create anxiety in her. She pushed and pushed for an answer since these disappearing acts were continual. He finally began to answer some of her questions. It was a marathon thirty-six hours of hammering away at him, almost begging him to come clean, and he finally did. He finally admitted the truth. He asked her to marry him only because he wanted to please her, but he told her he was not going to show up on the wedding day! He was going to leave her waiting at the altar!

He admitted he was filled with anxiety but would rather not hurt her by raining on her wedding-planning parade. As the date grew closer, his panic was at a fever pitch, and so, in his skewed way of thinking, he thought it would be better to not ruin her joy in planning her wedding. He thought it would be better to just leave her standing at the altar instead of manning up and telling her the truth.

Thank goodness she pushed and listened to her intuition. She was able to gain enough courage to break it off with him, cancel the wedding — and, sadly, lose a lot in her down payments for the venue and the caterer!

Marty

Marty was a lovely gentleman who was terribly commitment phobic. He would sabotage every good relationship that came along.

He finally ended up in my office because he was so lonely and depressive. He said, "I've got to find out what the heck is going on with me. I keep letting all of these amazing women go." With this statement I knew he was teachable and not narcissistic.

Many people who are commitment phobic may have narcissistic tendencies with little regard for the people they are hurting and don't really want any therapy for their patterns and behaviors.

But those who want to heal and understand and attend seminars and therapy are not narcissists. They are commitment phobic and come from difficult childhood situations, and without therapy, they just can't seem to help themselves.

Marty became panic stricken every time the woman in his life got comfortable, had needs and became human. As soon as she expressed her needs, he felt too much pressure was on him to please her and help her.

He never felt he had the right to say no.

Clearly, he had to do some deep work on his codependency as well. But for him, the woman's needs were a reminder of his childhood, in which his mother played the victim in a difficult marriage with his alcoholic father.

From a very early age, Marty had to cope with situations that were far too adult and complicated for his young mind and emotions.

Yet he was the only one whose thinking was clear enough to be able to solve the situation.

He was frequently woken up in the middle of the night by his agitated mother, who needed him to come with her to the bar to pick up his father who had passed out or was in jail due to his drunken belligerence.

Marty's sister had developed a terrible cutting disorder (a self-injurious behavior often associated with depression and anxiety) due to the unstable home life as well, and by the time Marty was sixteen, he had had a lifetime of caretaking the needy women of his life, and he felt he was done with this kind of relating.

Simply put, Marty had confused healthy emotional needs with toxic overneediness.

As his relationships evolved, Marty would nitpick and compulsively find fault. He was building a case for how bad each woman was so he could give himself the complete freedom to walk away.

He was a bona fide commitment-phobe; however, with a good amount of therapy to help him with his family-of-origin trauma, he eventually healed to the point where he was able to settle into a long-term, happy and committed relationship.

Marty worked on what I could call his post-traumatic stress disorder (PTSD) that came from his traumatic childhood.

He worked on his anxiety so that he was able to get into "right" thinking as opposed trauma-based anxiety, or "cut-and-run!" thinking.

Marty was able work on his unrealistic pickiness that had made him vilify perfectly good women.

With this kind of work, he was able to overcome his commitment phobia, which helped him to rewire his relationship-culture so that he was able to comfortably be in a long-term committed relationship.

Commitment-Phobe Traits
- Constantly giving mixed messages
- Always having one foot out the door
- Being aloof and hard to pin down
- Finding fault in the other person
- Building a shopping list of problems — nitpicking and criticizing
- Feeling trapped as soon as the other person gets too comfortable
- Having a tendency to cheat, lie and make up stories
- Being inconsistent and displaying push-pull behavior — the person is there and in love, and then they are not
- Feeling obliged and anxious because of another person's needs and having a profound desire to escape

Quick Tips for the Commitment-Phobic Person
- Practice meditation regularly as a way to calm anxiety. Escaping intimacy is often used as a means to calm anxiety; if this is the case, meditation can help to calm the feelings that lead you to sabotage your relationships.

- Work on being in the present moment; be right here, right now with the person in front of you. See what is good and right in the relationship now! (This is especially important for those of you in your child-bearing years who want to start to build a life with somebody.)

- Know and accept nothing and no one is perfect!

- If your family was dysfunctional, become aware of how your parents behaved and find ways to do the opposite.

- If you are the adult child of an addict or alcoholic who suffered under the volatility of your family, then consider going to ACA (Adult Children of Alcoholics/Dysfunctional Families) meetings. This may help you to share in a safe group setting with others who have gone through the same traumas that have contributed to such patterns as commitment phobia.

- Read the book *He's Scared, She's Scared: Understanding the Hidden Fears That Sabotage Your Relationships* by Steven Carter and Julia Sokol.

- Work to be honest with the person you are in a relationship with. Remember that lying is worse and more painful than knowing and sharing the truth.

- Decide that not leading anyone on is a rule you live by.

- Engage in therapy so you have someone to confide in and can learn more about yourself and your patterns.

Part III

Setting Boundaries

"Culturally, we find it difficult to say no. We are taught to be accommodating. Women particularly seem to struggle with empowering their "no" without feeling guilty. But men are not immune either. The reality is, without boundaries, you are likely to lose your real self, your autonomy and your well-being in any relationship."
- Victoria Lorient-Faibish

Chapter 6
The Key to Healthy Relationships

Good boundaries are the key to a good relationship-culture and are the underpinning of a good relationship with yourself and others. The art of knowing who you are, when to say no and when to say yes is the foundation. If you frequently feel angry, frustrated, resentful, guilty, taken advantage of, pushed or rebellious in relationships, these are signs and symptoms that you have boundary issues.

Those feelings would not show up if you felt at ease with boundaries and within your right to set a boundary in a firm but gentle way. Feeling and behaving like a hostage in a relationship is a common feeling when boundaries are unhealthy. People act in ways to avoid anger or conflict of any sort. With poor boundaries, relationships become a scary place, where people cannot relax and be genuine.

Isolation becomes a preferred mode of self-protection. Conversely, clinging and doing whatever the other person wants can also occur. I believe that boundary dysfunction is a major culprit in a person's feeling dissatisfied with their life. Unhealthy boundaries are self-defeating, unhealthy and the road to an unhealthy relationship-culture.

Culturally, we find it difficult to say no. We are taught to be accommodating. Women particularly seem to struggle with empowering their "no" without feeling guilty. But men are not immune either. The reality is, without boundaries, you are likely to lose your real self, your autonomy and your well-being in any relationship. Clients who come to see me to work on the unhealthy boundaries in their relationships are exhausted from the trap they find themselves in. They feel caught between knowing they need to change the imbalanced dynamic and feeling crippling guilt and fear at the prospect of activating their desired boundaries and stating their preferences. The codependence they feel has a tremendous grip on them. Their self-esteem rises and falls based on the other person's opinions, moods and tone of voice.

Their emotions and limits are subjugated to other people's wants and needs, or, conversely, they are constantly invading other people's boundaries as well due to their ignorance of what appropriate boundary negotiation looks like. Their low sense of self-value has the subconscious agenda of doing whatever the other person wants in order to not be abandoned and to be accepted.

In therapy, people get incredibly anxious when I start to talk about saying no to others or about telling someone that what they are doing is not acceptable behavior. People say, "I can't tell my mother/father/boyfriend/girlfriend/best friend that! They'll either hate me, be volatile or freeze me out, or I'll feel guilty and do anything not to feel that awful feeling of guilt — anything!" There is a deep fear that there will be a negative consequence to the boundary-setting experience. This is a normal reaction, especially if you've been trained by your family-culture, where no one valued the notion of setting boundaries. Remember, family-culture is brought down to us multigenerationally. It's something we inherit. It's the patterns, habits and ways of being that we absorb that influence our personalities and ways of dealing with people to form our relationship-culture. If you come from a family-culture that has no sense of good boundary expression and management, it is likely that you will have boundary problems later in life. We imitate what we are modeled in the family.

Let's say your family is one that does not provide a forum where it is safe to have feelings or express them, chances are you will stifle most of your own feelings as well. You may even become adept at numbing out your feelings as a way of coping. This is then parlayed into numbing out and eventually becoming unaware of your own opinions and points of view. It is a journey of shutting oneself down bit by bit. Conversely, you may feel you are the black sheep of your family, unable to shut down, but since you are not taught to express in a healthy way, the expressions will usually come out in violent outbursts of rebellion.

Finding Your Boundaries

The first and most important way to have a relationship that includes healthy boundaries is to be clear about how you feel about what you need and want. The habituation of having poor boundaries results in the numbing of one's true wants and needs.

There is a loss of the important clues that feelings provide that eventually generate a boundary. Instead of need and wants, other strong feelings show up; for example, constantly feeling angry, frustrated, hurt, resentful, boxed in, pushed, rebellious or victimized in a relationship is a sign that there are boundary issues in that relationship. Pay attention to what you are feeling. Don't just rationalize it away!

Do as much introspective work as possible. Slow everything down and observe your thoughts and feelings. Journaling is wonderful. Quiet breathing is wonderful. Good therapy is a useful tool to help a person slow it all down. Quietly meditating with your eyes closed is necessary for having an inner dialogue with yourself and asking yourself questions — "What am I feeling about this person? About me? About this situation?"

105

If you are so numbed-out to these signs and symptoms, you will not realize that your inner dialogue is trying to help you. Don't numb it out! You cannot constantly shut down your true nature, your true needs and your true self in a bid to be liked and accepted by the other. Understanding this at a deep level is when the journey of finding out what your boundaries are begins.

You Cannot Control Another Person's Feelings

It is difficult to simultaneously set a boundary and take care of another person's feelings. It would be like putting your feet on the gas and the brake pedals at the same time; you would go nowhere. As best you can, try to say to yourself, "I'm going to draw this boundary fully knowing the other person will react, but I'll try to do it fairly, kindly and lovingly. Then I will have played my part."

Partners, family members and friends may balk and have an issue with your drawing boundaries, especially if you never have in the past. They may say, "Who is this person? Is this someone new?"

They may feel that you are controlling them, or that you're being mean and have changed. That's fine! Trust that a new normal often has to come forth as you discover your self-culture, which includes the fact that you have a *right* to draw boundaries.

I repeat: You cannot control another person's feelings. However, you can control the way you deliver the message. Work to be as fair, kind, loving, compassionate and gentle as you can when you go about setting boundaries because if you set a boundary angrily or are manipulative, your message will essentially be lost in your manner of expressing it.

106

Draw Boundaries Outside of the Trigger Situation

If you try to tell your partner, "I don't want you to shame or humiliate me publicly," don't do it while you are in public! Meet in a private place and ask your partner not to do that. If you're in bed and you want to shed some light on a sexual boundary, wait and make sure you do it outside of the bedroom so that you are in neutral territory. This is the technique to use if you want to be heard and have the best chance possible for a positive outcome.

What Are Good Boundaries?

By definition, a boundary is the line we draw between ourselves and others to protect our emotional and physical space. Setting proper boundaries is important to our mental, emotional, physical and professional health. When we don't set appropriate boundaries, we run the risk of becoming resentful, depressed, overwhelmed and inauthentic.

When poor boundaries are in place in a relationship, the relationship becomes messy, and we can end up being too detached, overself-protective and isolated from others, or too dependent and overenmeshed with them.

It is important to remember that setting boundaries is not about controlling your loved ones. The people you are setting boundaries with may say you are, but they are just not used to your more empowered and vocal side. Drawing boundaries is more about defining what is acceptable to you and letting others know about it in a peaceful, clear and decided way.

Consistency is a crucial aspect of sending a clear message that a new dynamic is taking place. Also, very little will change if you set a boundary and then don't follow through. And remember, you are responsible only for your own feelings. It is important to disinvest from the outcome of a boundary-setting moment. You cannot please everyone all of the time.

Setting Good Boundaries:
- Move step by step into intimacy. It is important to check for compatibility before you reveal all the intimate details about yourself and your background. It is usually best to reveal only a little of yourself at a time.
- Say yes only when you want to. Say no when you want to as well.
- Don't operate out of guilt or manipulation.
- You have a right to your anger, but you need to express it in responsible and respectful ways.
- Do not to get caught up in the disease-to-please.
- Personalize your self-care. Find out what you need and desire, then take personal responsibility for it. You are the expert on yourself.
- Do not to make the other person responsible for your happiness.
- Check within yourself to see if you are falling for the person just because they are reaching out to you. If you do this, it may indicate that you are not looking at your own value and worth in a bid to avert loneliness.
- Commit to being true and authentic to yourself at all times. This may mean risking letting someone go. But waiting for the right person to fall in love with is so rewarding and definitely worth staying the course of commitment to self. Remember that like attracts like, and when you are in the vibration of self-love and self-respect, you are bound to attract a similar vibration in someone else. Have the intention to be true to yourself.
- As the relationship evolves, pay attention to what the other person is doing versus what they are saying.

"Show, don't tell" is the philosophy. Believe people when they *show* you who they are. Don't slip into a blissful oxytocin-induced denial of what is really going on. You really can't trust words in a new relationship. It's all about actions.

- Do not ignore the signs and symptoms of key warning flags.
- Don't fall in love with someone's potential! Pay attention to what you see in the here and now. Staying in a relationship based on what you think the other person *may* become is a tremendously tempting hazard that usually seriously disappoints.
- Stay true to your own core values despite what someone else may want; otherwise, feelings of self-betrayal may ensue. Compromise is needed in many areas as the relationship becomes more serious, but it is crucial to be the person you truly are versus whom you would like to present, especially at the beginning.
- Don't bring old patterns of behavior into the new relationship. Emotional projections and baggage from past hurts or past failed relationships can sabotage the future of a new and emerging connection.

The reality is that we grow the most through relationships. New ones are a worthwhile risk that needs to be taken with your eyes wide open.

Lessons will be learned no matter what, but the above guidelines may facilitate the navigation of the new relationship journey with a little more ease.

Unhealthy and Healthy Boundaries

Following are examples of unhealthy and healthy boundaries to help you determine where you might need to make changes to improve your relationships.

Unhealthy Boundaries

1. I reveal everything about myself when I first meet someone.
2. I trust no one, or I trust everyone.
3. I think in black and white and amputate people who disappoint me from my life.
4. I am overly generous to others so they will like me. I give beyond my ability.
5. I don't notice when someone invades my physical and emotional boundaries.
6. I allow others to direct my life, abandoning my values to please others.
7. I get mad when others do not fulfill my needs.
8. I expect others to anticipate and fulfill my needs.
9. I am volatile when I get angry.
10. I have trouble and often get confused when making decisions.
11. I walk around on egg shells.
12. I fall apart, so someone can rescue me.

Healthy Boundaries

1. When I meet someone new, I make sure we are compatible before I reveal intimate aspects of myself. I take my time in deciding to let someone enter my world.
2. I trust people appropriately and take my time with that process.
3. I live in the gray, moving bit by bit into an intimate relationship. I understand people have flaws as well as virtues.
4. I give only when I choose to give.
5. I respect myself.
6. I don't use generosity as a tactic to manipulate others to like me.

7. I notice and speak out when others invade my physical and emotional boundaries.
8. I am the master of my life. I maintain a sense of my own values no matter what others are doing. I know my own truth and inner voice.
9. I know I have the right to ask others to fulfill my needs. But I also know they have a right to say no. I am gracious when others say no to me.
10. I have a right to my anger, but I know I always express my anger in responsible ways.
11. I know what is right for me. I am clear and grounded. I trust my decisions.
12. I avoid having expectations of others. I take care of myself. I treat myself as a kind and loving parent would treat me.
13. I rescue myself.
14. I say yes only when I want to.

The Cycle of Self-Denial

Very often I see clients who, because of their family-culture patterns, enter relationships and end up in marriages operating from the paradigm that their own needs are low in their hierarchy of priorities.

They suffer from the disease-to-please and codependency and have an inner belief that their needs are not valid at all. This sets up a cycle of self-denial that leads to resentment, anger, rage and depression, which usually results in a broken marriage when that pattern finally erupts into bouts of rage in an unbridled bid to get one's needs met.

A model I often use in my office to explain why people might suffer from boundary issues (and codependency since the two are intertwined) is the "Cycle of Self-Denial" (next page).

The Cycle of Self-Denial:

I begin to express my needs but they come out in an angry raging manner!

Raging
- **Internal Raging:** Shows up as depression, victimhood, self-pity

- **External Raging:** Shows up as blinding anger and violent outbursts

But being human means I have needs!

- See me
- Hear me
- Understand me
- Love me
- Care about me
- What about me?

The Cycle of Self-Denial

- The valid message of my needs gets lost when I express my needs via anger
- I feel rejected when others do not respond positively to my needs and wants
- This leads me to believe that I should not express my needs

STARTS HERE!

- I feel I have no needs that I feel I can express
- I consider my needs to be "selfish"
- My needs are low priority
- My needs and wants are not important
- I feel guilty and ashamed when I express my needs
- The needs of others are always more important than mine

Anger and the Cycle of Self-Denial

The cycle of self-denial chart illustrates how denying your needs can lead to anger.

So often I have seen people who are so used to not asking for what they need — and don't even acknowledge that they have needs — that they reach a state of self-denial. "I don't have needs," they say, and usually they can pull this off, but at great cost to themselves.

At first they keep their needs to themselves and don't express them to anyone. They consider it selfish to be thinking of what they want.

Their needs are low on their priority lists, and if they do express their needs, they feel guilty and ashamed. But, of course, as time progresses, their basic human needs — to be seen, heard and understood, and to feel fulfilled — start to bleed through.

They begin to experience a sense of incongruity — a fight between "I don't want to admit that I have needs" and "I have needs."

What usually occurs next is that they either internalize their rage or express it outwardly.

Internal raging often results in depression, anxiety and a deep sense of dissatisfaction with themselves and their lives, which drags down their self-esteem.

External raging is exactly that: anger expressed outwardly, often in violent outbursts; it is frustration from a place deep inside that has come to the boiling point.

Whether their rage is internalized or expressed outwardly, these people send out undesirable energy, and they are difficult to be around. The fact that they have needs gets lost in their rage, and the world responds to them by saying, "I don't want to have anything to do with you," and as a result, their needs are never met, and they feel rejected and abandoned; they lose friends, become lonely, and their self-esteem and feelings of self-worth hit rock bottom.

Often when a person's self-esteem is lowered, they say things like, "I don't deserve to have needs," "I don't have value" and "I'm not worth much." So guess what? The cycle of self-denial begins all over again.

When learning to work with boundaries, this destructive cycle that was learned early in life needs to be stopped in its tracks. The first step is awareness and the second is to begin to express one's needs in an emotionally disciplined manner.

Vulnerability: Healing the Cycle of Self-Denial

I encourage people to get in touch with the vulnerable aspects of themselves. Good boundaries are best served when expressed as "vulnerable requests." This way, the communication is more likely to be delivered fairly, kindly and lovingly so people will be more receptive. People ask me if it is possible to be vulnerable without being in their "hurt child." I say, "Absolutely!" When a person is firmly planted in their "balanced adult," they are not playing the victim or manipulating. They are tapping into their softer side, coupled with their empowered side, which often yields a better result.[1]

---

[1] Victoria Lorient-Faibish, *Find Your "Self-Culture": Moving from Depression and Anxiety to Monumental Self-Acceptance* (Toronto: MASSenergy Press, 2014), 75–76.

Sometimes one has to be forceful in drawing boundaries, but most often I believe it is the quality of vulnerability that yields the best results when learning to effectively draw boundaries.

The key is to assess the situation correctly and to learn the most skillful manner to communicate with the people in your life.

This means that one does not always need to use a hammer to push in a thumb tack. Sometimes a gentle push is all that is needed.

Understand that drawing boundaries is not about controlling or harming the other person. It is the art of defining what is acceptable to *you* and letting others know about this in a vulnerable, peaceful, clear and decisive way.

Change begins with awareness, but it takes *awareness* plus *courage* plus *persistence* to bring about real change.

To create change, new neural pathways, new ways of thinking, new ways of relating — new self-culture-oriented living — you need to be courageous enough to say, "I'm aware that this is happening, and I have the courage to declare that to myself."

Through repetition and persistence, slowly go about the business of changing the patterns so you create a new normal within yourself.

If you are caught in the cycle of self-denial, then you must first know that it is right, good and healthy to have needs, and then to find peaceful, loving, fair ways to express those needs.

The needs do not have to be obscured by inner or outer rage. Even if you have been trained not to express your needs, it is important that you know that you have a right to have your needs satisfied.

And even though you have a right to express your needs, *it is not the responsibility of others to fulfill them.* You can lob the tennis ball over to the other side, and there is a 50-50 chance it will come back. Emotional self-sufficiency is important to remember here.

I invite you to practice a visualization to help you heal the cycle of self-denial. See appendix C, "Visualization to Heal the Cycle of Self-Denial." This exercise, when practiced often, can help you to rewire your neural pathways from this pattern.

Your Bill of Rights

As people start to heal the cycle of self-denial and start to build their self-esteem, I love to give them this list, which I adapted from a number of sources. I invite you to read these often:

1. I have the right to be my authentic self.
2. I have the right to have and experience my feelings.
3. I have the right to feel anger and to express it in responsible and constructive ways.
4. I have the right to say no, without explaining or feeling guilty, when I feel something is not right or I feel unsafe.
5. I have the right to make vulnerable requests of others. They may not fulfill my requests, but I have a right to ask.

6. I have the right to not feel bad or guilty just because another person doesn't like me or what I do, say, think or feel.
7. I have the right to have boundaries and to set limits in a fair and kind way.
8. I have the right to stick to my values and to honor my integrity.
9. I have the right to speak up when I think others are manipulating me or treating me unfairly.
10. I have the right to change my mind.
11. I have the right to be imperfect.
12. I have the right to make mistakes, to be unsure and to say "I don't know" without feeling guilty, dumb or stupid.
13. I have the right to not be affected by the opinions, tone or behavior of others.
14. I have the right to take full responsibility for my life.
15. I have the right to be joyful, healthy and confident.
16. I have the right to embrace and live my self-culture, even though it may be different from my family-culture.
17. I have the right to rewire my relationship-culture so that I can live a sane, healthy and joy-filled life.

Good Boundary Communication

Sometimes the words are just not there if you haven't practiced or been taught how to set good boundaries.

Here are some examples of sentences you might use to create a good boundary when negotiating in a relationship:

- That sounds like a good idea, but I'm just not ready to do this at the moment.
- I'll give it some thought.

- This really does not work for me. I would prefer...
- I need time to consider what you are asking me to do. I'll get back to you tomorrow on that.
- I would appreciate your not yelling at me when you are angry. I'll listen to you if you speak calmly to me.
- I ask that you please lower your voice.
- I feel _____, because I think _____.
- When you speak to me like that, I feel belittled, judged and criticized.
- If this continues, I won't participate in this conversation. (And follow through!)
- This is all I can take on. This is my limit.
- Please communicate with me calmly and honestly when we disagree. I simply won't participate in violent communication.
- I need to leave now. I'll speak to you later. (And make sure you do call at a later date.)
- I'm not ready yet. I need more time.
- This is who I am.
- I need to take time out from this discussion. I will be available to talk about this in an hour/day/tomorrow.

Baby steps at first are the name of the game. With time, good boundaries will be a real part of your life.

A new normal is just around the corner. Be consistent. Be good to yourself.

You need to fill your own cup first and create a strong, vital energy within yourself, and then you can give to others only from the overflow.

Part IV

Premarriage

"I urge people to work on their self-care so that they don't need the other person to change so they can feel okay. The most successful couples allow their partners to be just who they are without any pressure to change. If the way the other person is creates some discomfort in you, first try to look at yourself to see whether or not you can fill your own cup without making the other person be just like you."
- Victoria Lorient-Faibish

Chapter 7
Premarital Checklist

Before a couple makes their relationship permanent, I feel it is incredibly important that they look deeply at anything that might impact their union. One of my favorite endeavors is to work with clients who are about to be married and want to be on the same page regarding everything that pertains to their marriage to ensure that their relationship-culture remains healthy. I think this work is essential since, in my experience, so many couples end up in couples' therapy because they did not do this kind of due diligence early on. In a premarital couples' session, I ask the couple key questions to help them look deeply at their thoughts, feelings and habits with respect to various important areas of their lives.

Over no more than three or four sessions, we, as a team, tackle key areas to make sure neither party has a blind spot. Some revelations are uncovered during these sessions as we get crystal clear about where each person stands regarding subjects such as (1) money, (2) children, (3) family-culture, (4) sex, (5) communication, (6) family relationships and (7) lifestyle. These premarital sessions are essential in helping a couple who is heading toward a more serious and committed relationship.

Getting real about why you chose this person, what your inner motivations are and what your family-culture influences may be are so important to ensure a successful marriage and relationship-culture. In premarital therapy, I ask couples to mine their thoughts and feelings in the above seven key issues.

1. Money
One of the areas that seems to be incredibly difficult for couples to tackle, and which can eventually lead them through a maze of difficulty, is money. It is important for couples to get on the same page about money since in it is a vibrational essence that profoundly impacts their relationship-culture. I believe that the area of money has to be tackled head on and efficiently brought out of the realm of denial.

Ideally, I would like to see both people in the couple have the same attitude toward debt, savings and spending habits. However, each person comes from a different background, and they will have grown up learning different attitudes about money. One person might have come from a family-culture that treated money with respect; they paid bills on time, budgeted for savings and lived within their means. The other might have come from a family-culture in which they learned that it was rude to talk about money. They may have learned that there is a hidden aura around money that they, later on in life, bring to their relationship-culture. Discussing money may cause that person to be defensive and gear them up for a fight because they feel somehow invaded and attacked. Regardless of background, money is an area that can dig a deep hole into an otherwise positive and loving relationship.

Following are some key questions about money that we explore in premarital sessions. If you are working with your partner on this and any other of these issues, I encourage you to separately write down your answers to these questions, and then get together to discuss and compare what you've written. If you find a conflict, make sure that you get some support to navigate through your differences. Please don't decide to do nothing; if left unprocessed, your differences will fester and eventually create major problems in your relationship.

- What did you learn from your parents, grandparents and other family members about money? What was their attitude toward money?
- What is your relationship with money, savings, investments and bank accounts?
- Do you have a plan around your money?
- Do you want to retain separate bank accounts?
- Do you want to have a joint account?
- What kind of debt are you in? And what are you doing about it?
- How do you feel about savings? Do you contribute to savings?
- How do you feel about spending? Do you use shopping to ease emotional issues?
- What are your financial priorities?
- What are your financial goals?

Case Study

Trudy and Cameron, both in their late twenties, came in to see me for a few premarital sessions. Trudy had done some good work with me before on her issues with anxiety and learning how to speak up for herself in her job and in her relationship with Cameron. I had never met Cameron, but since Trudy had had such a positive experience with me before, he agreed to come in for three sessions to explore the topics around relationships and marriage and, at Trudy's request, some blind spots they might have that could lead to problems in their relationship later on. We discovered that one of their blind spots was how they both dealt with money. This was an area that they had not discussed at all. They both tackled the area quite individually, and Trudy was concerned that their lack of communication about this important topic would eventually negatively impact their relationship.

Trudy came from a family-culture that was generous with money, and her family taught her that saving was very important and that money was to be respected. She always paid her bills on time and felt anxious when she found out that Cameron did not. It wasn't that Cameron was careless, but paying bills on time was not always a priority for him. He also didn't realize how this could impact his credit rating, as well as Trudy's. Cameron came from a family-culture that just did not talk about money. In fact, he basically taught himself everything he knew about money. He understood the value of hard work because his parents were hard workers, but he was never taught about saving or about having a healthy relationship with money.

Trudy and Cameron had begun living together about a year before their engagement, and they were still getting their bearings living as a couple. Trudy was an avid saver for things she was passionate about, such as travel. Cameron spent money easily on electronics, and he frequently used his line of credit without letting Trudy know. Trudy was happy to be able to discuss this during our sessions, and I was able to mediate their dialogue so that the information would be delivered in a way that would not get Cameron's back up. I framed it in a way that would have both Trudy and Cameron wanting to be on the same page regarding how they dealt with money so that their financial future would be healthy and promising. Cameron wanted to make sure that we didn't completely disregard the value of spontaneity, yet Trudy wanted to make sure that they were both able to set up habits and patterns around money so that they could save to eventually buy a house. As Cameron began to realize that Trudy's goals were ones that he valued as well, the process soon became much easier. In our discussions, we made sure that they could create some room for free and spontaneous spending without adversely impacting their budget. This way, Cameron didn't feel that we were trying to deprive him of his freedom. Instead, he realized that this was a moment in time in which he needed to start to behave differently from the way he had previously around his finances.

Many other topics were broached in our three sessions, but the main accomplishment was coming up with a system that they both could live with regarding their finances. They decided that they would get one common bank account, but also retain their own personal bank accounts. They would use this common account to pay for their rent and common expenses. And with a common account, they could both see what was happening with their deposits and withdrawals. Trudy felt more at ease as she could see when bills were paid, and Cameron felt more at ease as he had his own personal account that he could dip into as needed without consulting Trudy for every little expenditure.

He was able to retain some spontaneity and freedom without impacting the larger budget that they had agreed on. They also set up a separate savings account in which they could build toward something they both valued, such as a trip or a down payment for their home. This discussion relaxed both of them as money was no longer an area of contention or a blind spot that could later negatively impact their marriage. They now had a method for negotiating their finances throughout their lives, and they were both able to get what they needed.

When couples do this kind of foundational work before getting married, they are less likely to engage in patterns and habits that eventually build resentment and walls that could lead to the demise of their relationships.

2. Children

Thoughts and attitudes about children are important to tackle before getting married. Believe it or not, many people do not discuss this subject honestly, and they end up finding, when they are married, that they are on opposite sides of the spectrum.

Following are some essential questions and areas to explore before you tie the knot.

• Ask each other directly, "Do you want kids?" And if the answer is yes, ask, "When do you want to start having them?"

For women who want children, this important topic needs to be explored and delved into deeply. The childbearing years are short and precious, and I strongly urge women who absolutely want children in their lives to not waste time with a person who does not. Couples who don't discuss this clearly before marriage are headed down a rocky road.

I am reminded of a couple I worked with for marital therapy who were not on the same page regarding children and ended up in a difficult and ugly conflict when the woman accidentally got pregnant. When they discovered she was pregnant, she wanted to keep the baby, but he did not. He said he wasn't ready to have children and wouldn't be for a long time, but she was already heading into her late thirties and was not willing to let go of this pregnancy. But because the pregnancy was a fact, they fell into the romantic notion that they could make it work after all; however, their lack of planning and foresight ended in profound emotional dysfunction. They came to see me for "rescue marital therapy" to see if they could save their marriage, but by this time, the child was already five years old, and they were already close to the demise of their relationship—and already holding a searing disdain for one another.

It always saddens me to see situations like this because it is the children who suffer the most. For me, as a relationship therapist, disdain, disrespect, resentment and disgust are always telltale signs that the relationship is potentially beyond repair. Once they have taken root, these emotions in a relationship are difficult emotions to overcome. I strongly urge people to be aware of it when they are heading in that direction. If they are, then it is paramount that they quickly get some marital assistance, advice and counseling. If they don't, I fear a slippery slope down the road of profound anger and eventual separation will ensue.

- Who stays home with the kids? And what are your thoughts and expectations regarding the woman staying home with them?

This topic is not for every couple, but it bears exploring if they intend on having one of them stay home with their children. The fact that a couple is living a modern life does not mean they will handle childrearing in an equally modern way, as my case study below demonstrates.

- How do you feel about paternity leave, daycare, a nanny and having a family member help with the children? I am not saying that people need to be crystal clear before they marry on the finer details of childcare, but I consider the premarital sessions to be a forum to open up the key topics and get a sense of where each person stands on them. These topics may need to be fleshed out later on, as couples get closer to the important milestones and decisions of their lives.

- Are we both on the same page about saving for our future children's expenditures and education?

This is another area to consider with regard to finances and priorities and where to allocate those finances. The key lesson here is that couples do not ignore or go into denial over the "children conversation."

3. Family-Culture

When one enters the realm of long-term relationships and marriage, it seems that despite good intentions to not be influenced by their family of origin's dysfunction, the autopilot "marriage personality" seems to crop up. For example, when a "modern" man begins to think about and prepare to get married, he may suddenly find himself copying the habits he observed in his father. He may find himself expecting his future wife to carry the lion's share of the domestic duties. Or, conversely, a woman may find herself, despite her modern alpha-female professional life, putting pressure on herself to fall into line with the traditional female role she observed in her mother.

Case Study

I worked with a couple, both of whom were extremely modern people. They were well employed, educated and thoroughly modern in every way. Yet Raj was very much his parents' son. As the relationship became more serious and they were headed toward marriage, it became evident that he had started to feel more in touch with his very traditional values regarding women and their roles in marriage. They had been living together for two years, but none of this traditional value system had come to light in that time. They shared cleaning duties and cooking, and they both brought a similar amount of money to the table.

After they became engaged, his traditionalism began to grow, causing Sharmila to become uncomfortable. It was as if the engagement had triggered in him a whole set of family-culture values that had been lying dormant at the back of his mind. They started to discuss the future and the timing for having children, but soon their discussions turned into full-blown fights as Raj insisted that Sharmila was to quit her job and stay home with their children. Her career was taking off, and she was deeply ensconced in an upwardly mobile trajectory in her profession. They were both in their late twenties, but she had no intention of becoming pregnant for at least eight years. Raj wanted them to start trying for children within the next year or two.

They had been dating in such a modern and equality-based way that his traditional values truly blindsided Sharmila. When they started to work with me, these discussions were burning a negative hole in their relationship. During the sessions, we were able to flesh out his true thoughts about women and marriage and the roles each person plays in that institution.

We discovered that Raj's mother had been a stay-at-home mom, and his father brought home the money. This was the most familiar way to him. His father also wielded most of the power, and his mother tended to the needs of the father and all of the kids. As a first-generation Canadian, Raj was still carving out his own way of being. He was definitely caught between the two worlds. And even though he was very modern, the traditional values seemed like an old familiar rhythm within him that became louder as he headed toward the traditional institution called marriage. In the process of our premarital work, he realized how this was impacting his fiancée, and this made him want to rethink his whole value system.

It became important for Raj to not jeopardize his relationship with his beloved Sharmila with his traditional thinking. Through our sessions, we were able to clarify what was important to each of them and what they were willing to let go of. Sharmila was clear that she was not interested in subjugating herself and her career aspirations by having children so soon and by staying home with them. Her priorities for her career were something she wanted respected in her marriage. I let Sharmila know that it was important that a spirit of compromise permeate the sessions. She needed to be open to the fact that she and Raj were on a journey that was going to require compromise and flexibility on both sides.

Raj needed to tone down his traditionalism, and Sharmila needed to see if there were any areas where she could compromise. I pointed out that Sharmila could stay home during the maternity leave that her company would provide her with, and then they could negotiate on childcare after that time period. Raj felt a little more assuaged as he realized that his future child would have the undivided attention of their mother for a good year with the maternity leave. I also pointed out that Raj could apply for paternity leave with his company. Even though that idea was extremely foreign to him, he became open to discussing it.

In the end, they agreed and understood that the way they had been living before their engagement was what they had both come to love and respect about each other. They realized that they wanted to fight to hold onto that and not acquiesce to traditional family values. They realized that they wanted to continue with the division of chores, responsibilities and day-to-day dealings as they had done for the past two years. They wanted to continue to create their own relationship-culture, taking a little from their families and adding a lot of their own experiential learning to create an amazing personalized relationship-culture that they could both love and live with peacefully. They embraced the notion that they did want children, but they were not ready to engage in this next step for at least four years. This was a compromise, and it relaxed both Raj and Sharmila. The key piece here was that no one was forcing anyone into anything.

From my vantage point, this was a coming-of-age story for both of these people. In sessions, I witnessed their transition to becoming more balanced adults and more secure and confident in what they had learned and what they had experienced in their own adult lives. It was quite impressive and inspirational to see two people embracing their own self-cultures in addition to creating their own personalized relationship-culture.

4. Sex

And what about sex? Sexuality is an area of a relationship that can make or break it. I feel that this is an area that needs to be constantly and deliberately looked at and tended to.

As your relationship becomes more intimate, clearer communication is required. As you delve deeper into the creation of your relationship-culture, you need to know that sex is and will always be one of the most important glues in a relationship. Whereas sometimes people build bridges through talk and emotional sharing, others build bridges and closeness through sex and physical intimacy.

The better the sexual realm is, the better the relationship is, in my opinion. I urge couples to never take this area for granted and also to never allow it to go into the "dead zone," shall we say. Communication in this realm needs to be free and open and relaxed so that sex can be connected, open, free, nonjudgmental, communicative, sensual, imaginative, respectful and consensual.

Following now are some of the questions that I ask couples in premarital sessions:

- Are you both happy with the way you communicate about sex?
- Are there areas in your sex life that you feel need to be improved?
- Are you both comfortable with how often the other person initiates sex?
- Are you both on the same page as to the amount of sex you are having?

5. Communication

Communication is an interesting area that can create substantial damage if there a lack of clarity and consciousness about it. The way a couple communicates with one another will either build a bridge or build a wall. The premarital sessions are wonderful for making sure that the patterns of communication are healthy and that both people are able to feel emotionally safe as well as the freedom to be authentic. This is also a forum for looking at the concept of fighting fairly. Even though many couples who are in the premarital stage of their lives may not want to discuss fighting, conflicts and negativity, I feel it is important to look directly at these kinds of things. The topic of communication is foundational for the premarital sessions and needs to be clearly brought forth.

Following are some questions I would ask couples regarding their ways of communicating:
- How do you communicate with each other?
- Do you feel that the way you communicate with each other is healthy?

- Are there any areas that are not working in the communication realm that you feel you want to discuss?
- Are there any hurt feelings or resentments that you feel you need to hide because you do not know how to communicate your true feelings?
- When you have conflicts, do you both feel that you fight fairly?
- Do you feel that you need to edit how you speak to your partner?
- Do you feel emotionally safe with your partner?
- How do you show your love?
- How do you best process your issues?

Case Study

Mark and Peter had been dating for a number of years when they came to me for some premarital work as they were soon to be heading down the wedding aisle. They wanted to make sure they were on the same page about key topics. I noticed that they were very compatible in a great many areas. They both loved sports, animals, fashion and cooking. They seemed hot for each other, which is a good thing for me to observe in a couple who are about to get married.

But Mark was quite concerned about the way they communicated with one another. Mark was not a verbal person, and was much more introspective than Peter. He craved time alone and silence and would frequently get into his cave mode, in which he preferred not to be disturbed. This regenerated energy he lost at his very demanding job as a dentist. Also, whenever he felt any emotional turmoil, he needed to go into his cave and work on it on his own.

Peter, on the other hand, worked in sales and was quite extroverted. He thrived on verbally processing any emotional issues he had. He didn't need the kind of cave time that Mark needed. In fact, Mark's cave time felt to Peter as though he was being isolated from the very core of his fiancé's world, and often a fight would break out. Peter could not understand Mark's way of being.

Once Mark had his fill of his alone time, he would reach out to Peter to connect so they could spend quality time together. But by that time, Peter's feelings were so hurt that he would pull back, and it would be days before they could communicate freely and openly once again. This cycle happened repeatedly, and it worried them both.

In our sessions, we spoke at length about the fact that both Mark and Peter had different needs regarding frequency and style of communication. They were also both very different in the ways they processed their unresolved issues.

Through the therapy sessions, they both gained a heightened awareness of one another's ways, and they were able to feel profound compassion for one another. The deep love they felt for one another motivated them to not want to perpetuate the dysfunctional pattern. They were able to create a new normal in which they were able to feel a sense of understanding for each individual's way of navigating through their feelings.

This scenario is common in a great many couples. Understanding that we are not all the same is so important in understanding that you can't force the other person to be just like you. Part of the journey of creating your unique relationship-culture is to respect that each person has a different way of communicating their love to one another.

One person may need to express their love through words, poetry, emails and letters. Another person may want physical touch, such as a massage or caressing, as a way to feel spoken to at a deep level. Sometimes people want gifts to know that the other person cares for and loves them, others feel time spent together is what really makes them feel a sense of security and togetherness. One person may need alone time to regenerate; the other person may need to talk to people in order to feel full again. Getting to know each person's authentic way of being is the work that couples need to do upfront to establish a healthy relationship-culture.

It is worth mentioning that I urge people to work on their self-care so that they don't need the other person to change so they can feel okay. The most successful couples allow their partners to be just who they are without any pressure to change. If the way the other person is creates some discomfort in you, first try to look at yourself to see whether or not you can fill your own cup without making the other person be just like you.

This kind of mutual respect and acceptance breeds tremendous amounts of trust and ultimately makes for an amazing relationship-culture that will stand the test of time.

6. Family Relationships

Sometimes as the couple becomes serious, one person will be extremely at peace with their own parents and family, whereas the other person might not feel comfortable spending time with their own family at all.

This is an important conversation to have as you become more and more bonded. It is essential for the couple to communicate openly about how much time they want to spend with their families of origin and how much they are willing to allow input from both their families on key decisions of their lives.

Following are a couple of questions that I ask during a premarital session about this area:
- How often do you visit your families?
- Is there any contentiousness about this?

Case Study

Maria and Tony came to see me before they walked down the aisle, and Tony's family became very much front and center in our discussions. Tony's mother was a devoted, loving and very involved Italian mother who wanted to be a part of all of Tony's key decisions. And now that they were engaged, Tony's mother felt within her right to opine on most of the wedding-related conversations. Tony's relationship with his mother was a close one. He was her firstborn after all! Tony was not at all good at drawing boundaries where his mother was concerned, and Maria was becoming increasingly annoyed at how much he allowed his mother to be involved. If they didn't get this under control, it would become a real problem as their life as a couple evolved.

Maria was decidedly different from Tony with regard to her experience with her family. Her father had passed away when she was young, and her mother was a quieter sort of person who allowed her daughter to make her own decisions. Maria was not at all used to a matriarch making her presence known in this way. Maria spoke to her mother once a week and visited her approximately once a month. Tony, on the other hand, spoke to his mother daily and saw his parents weekly. Clearly, Maria and Tony were very different in their relating habits with their families.

The only way this was going to work was if Tony was willing to realize that his relationship with Maria had to become a top priority for him. (It is my philosophy that couples need to make each other the most important person in their lives after themselves. In other words, self-care is number one in that you need to fill your own cup first and give to others only from the overflow. Honoring yourself first is the only way to have truly healthy relationships. After yourself, your partner needs to be second on your priority list.)

This was not going to be easy for Tony, but, thankfully, he was willing to understand that Maria was the person who was going to be living with him and spending his future with him.

Stepping into his full adult self meant that his adult love relationship needed to be the main event in his life.

In our therapy sessions, we were able to come up with a compromise that didn't change Tony's daily communication with his mother, but they didn't spend every weekend with Tony's parents either.

Tony and Maria realized, through our work, that carving a new path together as a couple was not going to be easy in the face of such a strong family-culture, but it was going to be essential if they were to create their own unique relationship-culture.

7. Lifestyle

And finally, how each person wants to live their life is a key area that needs to be navigated in premarital exploration. You need to ask yourselves if you are both on the same page regarding the following aspects of your lifestyles:

- Living in an urban center versus a rural setting
- Living in a condo or house
- Living near family or farther away from family
- Having pets or no pets

- Having children or no children
- Being clean or messy
- Having a TV or no TV
- Being vegetarian or not
- Being religious or not
- Celebrating holidays with family or not
- Celebrating holidays at all
- Being traditional or modern
- Being health conscious or not
- Enjoying fitness and sports or not

Doing this kind of premarital exploration is the foundation of a healthy relationship-culture that can stand the test of time.

Finding and knowing one's unique relationship-culture is the most important endeavor a couple engages in as they become more committed and more serious.

When a couple defines their own relationship-culture, they are essentially laying the groundwork for the future. When they do this exploratory work, they are not living an unconscious, haphazard life.

As the couple connects in deeper ways, they are awakening to a life that is conscious and deliberate.

Relationship-culture is all about being able to live an authentic life together, while at the same time honoring each person's unique self-culture.

Knowing yourself fully is the key. A spirit of compromise is also important. Striking a balance between self and the relationship is what makes for a more healthy, functional and authentic relationship-culture.

Part V

Marriage

"But let there be spaces in your togetherness, and let the winds of the heavens dance between you. Love one another but make not a bond of love: Let it rather be a moving sea between the shores of your souls."
- **Kahlil Gibran,** *The Prophet*

Chapter 8
Relationship Rescue 911!

I'm someone who believes in marriage. I myself have been in a successful 20-plus-year marriage. I believe it's possible to have a healthy, happy and passionate marriage. Even though statistics today indicate the institution of marriage is rocky, I'm hopeful. I believe that often those who end up heading for divorce do so because they don't have the tools to navigate the sometimes rough waters of marriage.

People get bored and lack the emotional discipline to hang in there. Also, the advent of children is a challenge to a marriage and people don't have the tools to cope with this. They play out their family-culture dysfunction without knowing they're doing so. They have addictions and aren't getting help. They're codependent, enabling, overworked, exhausted, impatient, irritable, blame-oriented, feeling like the victim and living from their hurt-child perspective.

Gottman's Destructive Behaviors
John Gottman, a preeminent marriage researcher, discovered in his innovative research of forty years of monitoring couples that to maintain a good relationship, couples must generate five seconds of positive emotions for every second of negative emotions during conflict discussions.[1] This is because negative emotions have more power to hurt a relationship than positive emotions have to help. Negativity seems to make a stronger imprint on the brain, and we need to take action to continually counteract the negativity so that it does not tear a couple apart. Dr.

---

[1] Ellie Lisitsa, "The Positive Perspective: Dr. Gottman's Magic Ratio!" December 5, 2012, http://www.gottmanblog.com/sound-relationship-house/2014/10/28/the-positive-perspective-dr-gottmans-magic-ratio.

Gottman named four negative behavior patterns that can predict divorce. He called these destructive patterns "The Four Horsemen of the Apocalypse."[2, 3]

- **Criticism:** Passing judgments. Nitpicking. Constantly finding fault in the other person. Using "you" sentences; for example, "You need to go on a diet" or "You dress like a child." Using the words "always" and "never" in sentences describing your partner; for example, "You always think only about yourself," "You never do things the right way" or "You never do anything for me."
- **Contempt:** Feeling that the other person is inferior to you. Feeling that you are superior to the other person. Having no respect for the other person. Feeling disgusted with the other person; for example, saying, "What's wrong with you?" "You're disgusting!" "I can't believe I'm even with you."
- **Defensiveness:** The communication is coming from a perceived feeling of an attack. Feeling like the victim in the dynamics. Feeling as though you have to constantly protect yourself. The communication comes off as angry, corrective, protective; for example, "It's not my fault that we don't communicate well."
- **Stonewalling:** Completely shutting the other person out. Ceasing interaction with them. Emotionally amputating them. Ignoring them. Behaving as though they don't exist. Freezing the other person out as a punishment for not doing what you want them to do or behaving the way you want them to behave.

---

[2] The Gottman Institute, "Research FAQs: What Are the Negative Behavior Patterns That Can Predict Divorce?" 2015, http://www.gottman.com/research/research-faqs.
[3] John M. Gottman and Julie Schwartz, "The Empirical Basis of Gottman Couples Therapy," 2013, https://www.gottman.com/wp-content/uploads/EmpiricalBasis-Update3.pdf.

Gottman says that these behaviors predict that a couple will get a divorce at an average of 5.6 years after the wedding. Emotional withdrawal and anger predict that a couple will get a divorce at an average of 16.2 years after the wedding.[4]

In reality, marriage is tough, and yet I believe it is through being in a bonded relationship such as marriage that we can learn and grow so much. For many, it's tempting to not risk entering into the relationship realm for fear of being hurt. I observe people entering into a hyperself-protection mode and ending up becoming commitment phobic to try to avoid the hurt that marriage might bring.

Yet I am encouraged as a therapist to witness younger generations open to therapy and ready to move past their family-culture dysfunctions in favor of not repeating these behavior patterns. And what inspires and encourages me most is to watch relationships and marriages heal through the diligent act of working with the various important tools I discuss in this book.

I believe it is possible to have a successful marriage. I believe it is possible to define your relationship-culture so it's healthy, functional, respectful, sexy, passionate, fun, joyful, mutual and ever evolving.

The Child versus the Adult: Who's in This Relationship?

The Hurt Child in Action in Relationships
One of the most critical and important situations that influences and creates problems in long-term relationships and marriages is when one or both people in the relationship are coming from their hurt child. This could

---

[4] The Gottman Institute, "Research FAQs: What Are the Negative Behavior Patterns That Can Predict Divorce?" 2015, http://www.gottman.com/research/research-faqs.

also be the wounded child, the neglected child, the deprived child or the abused child. Whichever "child" is in action within a person, it is the unresolved child in the adult person playing itself out and wreaking havoc on the relationship or marriage. Can you imagine a hurt or deprived six-year-old running your marriage?

If dysfunctional love is all that person experienced, then that kind of love is normal to them and they will bring it into their relationships. This dysfunctional, unresolved, unconscious aspect of a person projects itself onto the marriage as a ticking time bomb. The hurt child carries the baggage of hurt and anger into their adult life.

To know what you are dealing with regarding an unresolved hurt child wreaking havoc on a marriage, you need to understand what that is all about. Most, if not all, of the issues that a couple faces when they need couples' therapy comes from this unresolved young child who is hurt and has run amuck without a way to deal with it appropriately. The inner child needs tools to heal and repetition of new, healthier behavior to unlearn the old patterns from the past that have surfaced in their adult life.

Examples of the Hurt-Child Behavior in a Relationship

- **Having affairs or addictions.** The hurt child is not able to sustain any sort of boredom. Often people who operate from the child in themselves seek out excitement through extramarital affairs or addictions that ultimately destroy the relationship if their issues are not dealt with. They may also maintain the extramarital affair or addiction as a secret for a long time, living a double life, which also promotes self-destruction and the demise of the relationship. They may feel, because their hurt child is unconsciously in action, that they deserve to constantly reward themselves with excitement as opposed to dealing with their quotidian life with their partner. The hurt child refuses to do the responsible thing and deal with the marriage in a healthy and integrity-oriented manner. This is an acting out of sorts that negates any good, adult-like decision making.

- **Playing the victim and the blame game.** The hurt child often acts like a victim so that someone will rescue them, always asking, "Why me?" or saying, "Poor me" as their core inner dialogue. The hurt child also falls apart so someone will take care of them. They refuse to take responsibility for their actions and emotions, blaming others and not taking responsibility for their own life decisions. The person's hurt child is a "comfort-addict."

When I work with couples who are having trouble in their relationships, I speak about this hurt-child and comfort-addict aspect as a major contributor to the possible demise of the relationship. The comfort-addict is unable to tolerate discomfort for any length of time; they impulsively need to leave things and situations quickly to numb out any uncomfortable feelings that they encounter. The hurt child can be found in any aspect of our adult lives, but it especially makes its presence known in our long-term adult relationships, particularly the ones that involve great responsibilities.

Inevitably, if the hurt child is not tamed and worked with and taught that emotional discipline is the key, the impulsiveness and inability to tolerate discomfort will wreak havoc on a long-term relationship, which can be filled with times of discomfort, as life sometimes is.

The comfort-addict seeks out behaviors that turn down the volume of real life.

- **Using guilt as a weapon.** The hurt child will use guilt as a way to manipulate others to do what they want them to do or feel what they think they should feel. Guilt is such a powerful weapon and will be utilized as a way to get what they need because they do not feel that they can get what they need in any other way. The hurt child often has an inner self-loathing and low self-esteem because they probably experienced a lot of criticism growing up. The compromised self-esteem and lack of a sense of self-value makes a person operate in desperate ways, such as inducing guilt to get what they need. The hurt child also, in turn, feels guilty indiscriminately; feeling blamed and ashamed unnecessarily are all the domain of the hurt child in action.

- **Being defensive.** And let us not forget defensiveness. The hurt child often feels ubiquitously attacked, which puts them on the defensive, so they correct others and aggressively put them in their place. This is a real relationship killer! Defensiveness is the way for the hurt child to overprotect themselves and overset boundaries because they don't feel they have any recourse.

- **Using sarcasm.** Similarly, sarcasm is a tool from the toolbox of the hurt child. Sarcasm comes from a deeply immature place, especially in the context of communication within a relationship. Sarcasm is passive-aggressive anger, and, as such, it leads to resentment. I often ban sarcasm from a couple's communication during their therapy since it is an unhealthy and childish way to express anger. Later in this chapter, under the heading "Technique for Couples' Communication: Initiate and Reflect," I talk about better ways to deal with conflict and anger.

- **Hiding under the disease-to-please and chameleon behaviors.** Disease-to-please behavior is the domain of the hurt child as well. An obsession with pleasing others is an unconscious strategy, learned in early childhood, to make sure others like them so that they are not abandoned. The sense of self is so poor that the disease-to-please pattern often makes the person into a chameleon, whereby they transform themselves into whatever their partner wants. The disease-to-please and chameleon-like behaviors keep the person from ever admitting that they are angry. This patterning certainly leads to resentment that builds within, only to explode on the scene in inappropriate ways, readily destroying the relationship.

More Hurt-Child Behavior

- Withdrawing emotionally from others without letting them know why.
- Expecting other people to be mind readers, and then getting angry at them when they don't know what's going on is typical hurt-child behavior.
- Having invisible boundaries. This unfair behavior occurs when a person has a line that should not be crossed, but they don't let the other person know about it. This boundary then gets inadvertently invaded because there was no clear communication about the boundary. This is fodder for many fights and disagreements.
- Having temper tantrums when they don't get their way.
- Being rebellious just to get back at the other person. This is actually an unresolved hurt teenager.
- Constantly feeling jealous. Jealousy comes from a profound lack of self-esteem that was probably generated early in a person's family-culture life.
- Being unable to set clear boundaries and always allowing others to invade their space and their boundaries.

- Always living in fear and panic and having no trust or faith in life.
- Taking people hostage with emotional blackmail.
- Feeling a deep emptiness inside; they feel they are "not enough" and that they "don't get enough."
- Obsessing with and focusing on the past; they constantly live in regret.
- Feeling that life is unfair.

Healing the Hurt Child

One of the tools that I use to help couples who may be acting out from their hurt child is a "reparenting" visualization. This visualization begins the rewiring of the neural pathways of the habituated hurt child who is destroying the relationship.

The hurt child is suffering because they didn't get what they wanted and needed from their parents or family-culture environment, and they project this onto their adult relationship or marriage. The only way to move beyond the scars of one's upbringing that are wreaking havoc on the adult relationship is for the person to understand that they need to reparent *themselves* so that they can feel full again and stop projecting their emptiness onto their partner. This visualization begins the process of giving themselves permission to appropriately make themselves a priority and to treat themselves as they wished they had been treated as a child. They need to learn to be kind, loving, compassionate and forgiving toward *themselves* to be able to do the same for other people.

With daily repetition and the resulting laying down of new neural pathways, this exercise allows a person to heal the wounds of the past. Only then will they be able to move into real adulthood with healthy relationships. Also, for the hurt child to no longer run the show, the child within needs to know that the adult has life well in hand in real terms. Only then can the child finally relax, knowing that the adult is making good decisions, drawing boundaries, doing the right thing and creating a safe environment. The acting-out child behavior is mainly a product of the adult not taking care of life in an adult and responsible fashion, so the child goes about the business of trying to survive, but does it in an immature, childlike way. If your relationship is suffering because of your or your partner's hurt-child behavior, I encourage you or your partner to practice the "Visualization to Reparent Yourself and Heal the Hurt Child" in appendix D.

Parentifying and Infantilizing Patterns of Behavior

We all, in fact, have at one time or another embodied the hurt child; we are flawed works in progress. Changing these dysfunctional states of being that create relationship dysfunction requires great awareness and a willingness and courage to change so these behaviors can be processed and neutralized. It's important to know when you take on the hurt-child voice, you attract the parent like a magnet into your relationship, and vice versa. Look around and you'll see this dynamic in relationships — one "parentifying" the other, and another "infantilizing" the other — each state of being feeding on the other. I have observed many couples who treat each other either like a parent or like a child, and then they ask me what might be the reason for their not being sexually attracted to one another. Nobody wants to have sex with their parent or their child! The parentification/infantilization dynamic is the fastest way to kill the sexual dynamic in a long-term relationship.

Case Study

John and Annie had been married for about ten years. They had two beautiful children whom they loved and adored. Annie was an organized, effective businesswoman who wanted her home to be run like a tight ship. John, on the other hand, was a prolific artist who loved to create and to daydream. He would fly kites with his children and delight in walks in nature, where they talked to grasshoppers and identified animals they detected in the clouds. Annie had a busy and successful business as a publicist, whereas John worked from home on his art, his photography and on his music album. He had investments from previous successful art shows that he attended to as well, so he was not completely out of the financial loop in the relationship. Yet it was Annie who brought in most of the money. There was no real resentment about the financial imbalance.

They came in to see me because their sexual relationship was waning, to say the least. They were also fighting a lot, and the marriage was seriously barreling like a freight train toward a brick wall with their constant bickering, criticizing and building resentment. They didn't want to separate since it was not financially feasible, nor was it something they wanted to put their children through since they had both come from family-cultures of divorce. As we dug into our therapy, what stuck out strongly was that Annie felt as though she had three children, not two. The resentment she felt was often what started their fights, and then John's needed to defend himself and often ended up storming out. They'd then spend days not talking to each other, which became a tortured atmosphere for the children.

What finally brought them to my therapy office was the fact their son was showing profound signs of anxiety, even though he was only eight years old. In his fits of crying, he'd scream that he couldn't stop worrying his parents were going to divorce. Their daughter was a more stoic, a holed-up-in-her-room-reading type, but her withdrawing was increasing, and John and Annie were worried about both their children and how their fighting was impacting them.

Through our deep therapeutic process, we found that Annie didn't feel supported in her marital life. She was the first to say that John was a wonderful father; however, she said that he didn't take responsibility for anything. She said responsibility was completely off his radar. Annie said that she was the only one who created the shopping and chore lists since John never thought about such things.

John said that every time he came up with a list or an idea, Annie criticized him and said his idea was either wrong or needed to change in some way. He felt as though nothing he did was ever good enough for Annie, and so he had given up trying to participate in those areas. He had chosen to abdicate from the areas that he felt would engender judgment and criticism toward him. He had come from a family-culture in which his mother criticized everything his father did, which made that a sensitive spot for him.

Initially, John and Annie had come together as a couple because of their mutual love for art and creativity, but with life and the evolution of financial responsibilities as well as children, Annie took on the role of the responsible parent, providing them all with a stable life equipped with routine and regularity. But that had taken a toll on her as she worked long hours and complained bitterly about coming home to a messy house and children who had so much sugar in them that they couldn't relax enough to have a calm bedtime routine. Many fights broke out within half an hour of her arriving home, which created a tremendous amount of stress around dinnertime as well as bedtime. She also complained that she was always seen as the bad guy since John refused, in Annie's estimation, to be a strong disciplinarian. This had all become a tremendous turn off for Annie because she felt that John didn't support her enough, and this impacted her attractiveness to him. She felt hurt, annoyed and resentful about this.

Annie had grown up in a home where routine and order were valued. Her mother and father were very organized people who demanded Annie and her siblings be organized and adult-like from a very early age. What Annie loved about John in the beginning was that he embodied the opposite of what she'd grown up with. With John, she'd been able to be childlike and creative, and for the first years of their marriage, before they had children, it worked very well, and their sexual and emotional passion was profound. As life became filled with bills, children, mortgages and taxes, Annie recognized the value of her family-culture teachings that had kept their lives sane and organized.

In therapy, John bemoaned the fact he couldn't understand why Annie no longer wanted to have sex with him. He said that he made a tremendous effort with the children and tried to make many romantic gestures, such as picking fresh flowers and creating warm lavender-scented baths for her, only to be rejected. But all this only caused Annie to feel more resentment since what she really needed was for John to become more of an adult and to get on the same page with her regarding the household routines and the children.

What had contributed to the deterioration of the sexual connection and ultimately put the marriage in danger? I can list seven problems: (1) Annie had changed with the changing landscape of the marriage and John had not. (2) Annie had given up on having any faith that John could be a participating adult in the marriage and had treated him like one of her children. She judged and criticized him and punished him with her silence. (3) They didn't have a good methodology for negotiating the conflicts they found themselves in. (4) John saw Annie as if she were his chastising parent and looked to escape, rebel and hide from her, often by retreating into his world of art and creativity. (5) Annie and John didn't trust each other, and now they were resentful of one another, causing immense walls to come between them. (6) Annie and John were not in their fully balanced adult selves, hence they had no desire to engage sexually with one another. (7) Annie infantilized John, and John parentified Annie.

Neither Annie nor John had any idea of the dynamic they had created that was particularly detrimental to their sex life and to their marriage in general. They had no awareness that they were in this parentifying/infantilizing patterning that was killing their relationship. The awareness of this became the key to changing most of their dysfunctional dynamics. As soon as Annie realized she was treating John like her third child, it became a watershed moment for her. And then as soon as John realized that he was treating Annie like he treated his mother, this too became a major aha moment for him that stopped him dead in his tracks and changed many of his choices. In therapy, we devised clear boundaries around what each person needed to do with regard to participation in the household and childcare duties. Thankfully, both Annie and John were committed to the marriage and staying together. This made it much easier to effect change and to penetrate the long-held patterns that they were both unconsciously activating.

Annie realized that she was not giving John a fair chance to do things his way. She owned up to the fact that she allowed herself to be undisciplined in her communication with John, whereby she would hurl unedited insults and judgments at him. And John also realized that he was acting in rebellious ways that contributed to the inflammatory and cyclical fights they would have. He owned up to the fact that he had abdicated from his duties as the adult parent in favor of being seen as the good guy by his children. He admitted that his self-esteem was low, and the validation he got from being friends with his children became something he unconsciously wanted to perpetuate, not realizing that this created a devastating imbalance in how the children saw the two parents—essentially pitting the two kids and their dad against Annie.

I encouraged Annie to work at being clear about what she needed from John. She would vent that she should not have to tell John what she needed, that he should know what she needed if he really loved her. John would then vent that he wasn't psychic and that she needed to learn how to ask for what she needed. I let them both know that they needed to be able to feel safe enough to ask for what they needed so they could build trust. They needed to feel confident that what they needed would be heard and honored. I also let them know that it was okay to ask for what they needed, but that there was a 50-50 chance that what they needed might not be fulfilled by the other person. There needed to be some freedom for a person to say no when they were asked for something in the relationship. In addition, in truth, the way they were asking things of each other was done in such offensive and disrespectful ways that no one was ever up for listening to the other. In the therapy sessions, both Annie and John were reined in regarding how they were allowed to speak to one another. I was able to teach them new ways of communicating that brought them into the realm of adulthood as opposed to throwing tantrums like children in adult bodies. It bears repeating that, within relationships, the most effective way to communicate what you want is to find your sense of vulnerability and make your requests from that vulnerable side of yourself. Vulnerability tears down the walls of resentment and creates an atmosphere in which both people feel emotionally safe with one another. As mentioned in chapter 6 regarding healing the cycle of self-denial, these requests are called "vulnerable requests." Annie and John learned to make a variety of vulnerable requests of each other. I also encouraged them to say no if they truly could not fulfill the request. This kind of freedom built a tremendous amount of trust in the relationship.

Annie and John also needed to apologize to each other for the nasty, mean and disrespectful things they had said to one another. They both acknowledged that being in therapy meant that they both cared enough about each other and their family to want to stay together. I encouraged them to remind themselves of what had brought them together in the first place. They needed to recapture that aspect of themselves so that they could be open to learning these new ways with one another, including how they communicated.

We set up date nights and family nights, and we also created a positive nighttime routine. I brought in some studies for John to read about how sugar impacts children, and so sugar no longer was part of their regular day-to-day nutrition. The children started to feel a sense of calm as Annie and John fought less often, and when they did have conflict, they used a technique that taught them to bring their adult selves quickly in line so that they could move through a conflict constructively. Through therapy we were able to create a new normal for this family. When this parentification/infantilization dysfunctional dynamic is active, there is an urgent need to stop it so that the relationship can be saved. Awareness is the key, and as Maya Angelou said, "When you know better, you do better." If you are aware, you can break the loop. When you move away from blindly repeating your behavior, you can move toward neutralizing the pattern.

Technique for Couples' Communication: Initiate and Reflect - *Working with Conflict and Anger in a Healthy Way*

The technique I used with Annie and John to immediately stop their dysfunctional fighting is called "Initiate and

Reflect." This technique is used in many conflict-resolution circles and has its roots in Carl Rogers' "client-centered" therapy.[5] It is a mirroring/reflecting exercise that promotes an atmosphere of emotional safety, acknowledgement and compassion. It also stops the overreactive and undisciplined communication dead in its tracks. This creates a set of rules for the couple to abide by if they're interested in promoting a healthy relationship-culture. Also, if the couple has children, it saves the children from having to live in a home of yelling and tension. Children who grow up in highly volatile home environments where there is much arguing become hypervigilant and filled with anxiety.[6]

Fighting without a proper communication technique is like traveling in a train heading toward a brick wall. It is a useless, dangerous, damaging experience. This is not to say one cannot acknowledge one's feelings, including anger. You have to acknowledge what you think and feel, but you need to do it responsibly. One needs to understand that everything a person experiences in a fight or as a trigger is *their* story and *their* movie. There is not one universal perspective. It is *your* movie, *your* version and perspective, of a situation; everyone else does not necessarily share it.

The Initiate-and-Reflect technique that I use in the office, is a process of restating, mirroring and reflecting the speaker's feelings and words. The purpose of this technique is to give the time and space for the speaker to "hear" their

---

[5] Center for Building a Culture of Empathy, "Empathy Movement: Reflective Listening Links,"
http://cultureofempathy.com/projects/Empathy-Movement/References/Reflective-Listening.htm.
[6] Kathryn Doyle, "Parent Behaviors Linked to Kids' Anxiety, Depression," *Reuters Health*, December 13, 2013, http://www.reuters.com/article/2013/12/13/us-parent-kids-anxiety-depression-idUSBRE9BC0VR20131213.

own thoughts and to focus on what they want to say and feel. It also creates an atmosphere of goodwill that shows those involved in the process that everyone is doing their best to understand the other person. It also keeps the lines of communication open. This process does *not* involve asking questions, giving advice or introducing a new topic, nor does it involve leading the conversation in another direction. This is about helping both people to feel understood, acknowledged and heard. In this technique, the other person *listens* carefully to what the speaker is saying, and then they *mirror* what the speaker has said after the person has finished speaking, and, finally, the other person *empathizes* with the emotions that the speaker has disclosed.

Understanding versus Resolution

Sometimes this technique does not provide a resolution to a disagreement or problem, but does provide an atmosphere of emotional safety and the building of trust, which can be a resolution in and of itself. However, this can feel frustrating to the couple since sometimes people come from the perspective of needing to be right and want to impose their point of view on the other person. I encourage people to understand that, most often, finding a resolution to the problem should not be the main goal, and that everyone is entitled to their own feelings, perspectives and opinions in a situation. Nor is being in agreement the best goal. I feel the most useful goal for the couple in conflict is mutual respect and to listen to one another. This means both people are entering into their adult selves versus coming from the child self who is never logical or helpful to the relationship.

All this, rather than being in agreement and having the same opinion, needs to be the main objective. Sometimes the best we can do is to commit to not trying to control the other person by demonstrating that acknowledgment, respect and listening are the main focus and the priority.

The Technique
There are many variations to this technique, and as couples practice it and become more comfortable with it, they will be able to incorporate some of the variations. However, I believe that initially it is important to be diligent in sticking to the precise rules of the technique as I set them out here.

The Rules
- Who is the *initiator*? This is the person who has been triggered, feels hurt or angry and needs a forum to communicate.
- Who is the *reflector*? This is the person who will be listening and reflecting back what they hear.
- Each person in the couple will have the opportunity to be the initiator and the reflector.
- Asking for permission: It is important for the initiator, once triggered and wanting to engage in this exercise, to ask the reflector for permission to participate in the exercise. This is an act of respect for the other person's boundaries.
- The initiator would say, "I would like to initiate. Can you reflect?" This question needs to be a universal and clear sign for both parties that someone has experienced an emotional trigger or a problem in their interactions that needs to be fleshed out in a healthy and functional way. Both people need to know that to refuse to participate in the exercise is to allow dysfunction back into their relationship and for unhealthy fighting, reacting and sniping to continue.
- The reflector can say yes or no, but if no is the answer, they need to agree on a timeframe for when they will engage in the exercise. The answer can be "no, not now, but in an hour I can" or "no, not now, but tomorrow I

can." This is a goodwill gesture that says "I'm willing to participate in a healthy technique to avoid dysfunctional conflict. I respect that you have felt a trigger, and I'm willing to participate in a technique that will help us and this relationship to heal this problem."

The Key Sentences

As the initiator, you begin with a statement, told to the reflector, about what you are feeling—your story told from your perspective—so you begin with "I"; this is your movie, your viewpoint.

Initiator: "I feel _____ because I think _____." In this important initiating sentence, the initiator identifies a *feeling* they have, such as angry, hurt, confused, betrayed, frustrated, annoyed, ignored, abandoned, left out, irritated, surprised, resentful, fearful, sad, jealous, insecure or any other emotion they may be feeling because they *think*, from their perspective or in their imagination, that something has occurred to make them feel this way. For example, they might say, "I feel sad because I *think* you are ignoring me." The other person may not, in fact, be deliberately ignoring their partner. They may be distracted by some problem they are experiencing that may have nothing to do with their partner. However, the partner who is feeling ignored may be feeling sad, and this is something that needs to be brought up. It is important to keep the sentences short and clear. This way the couple can adhere to the specifics. It is important for the initiator to look deep inside to identify what they feel (to this end, I always recommend that the initiator write down their feelings first).

Reflector: "So, let me see if I got this right. You feel _____ because you think _____. Is that right?" (For example, in response to the sentence above, as the reflector, you would say, "So, let me see if I got this right. You feel sad because you think I am ignoring you. Is that right?"

With this, you choose not to respond defensively, which would surely negate the initiator's expressed feeling. Instead, you are simply listening, reflecting and acknowledging your partner's feeling. It is important here that no one can dispute the feeling of the other person. It is *their feeling*, and that is not up for discussion. You may not agree with your partner's feeling, and that is okay. You do not need to take on the other person's feeling; all you can do is listen and acknowledge that your partner has a particular feeling by reflecting their words back to them.)

Initiator: "Yes." (If no is the answer, then the initiator needs to make their statement again, and the reflector needs to reflect again. This should be repeated until the reflector has *accurately* understood what the initiator said.)

Reflector: "Is there more?" (If the answer is yes to both questions, then the initiator can begin again with a new sentence. This can continue for three or four sentences as the initiator delves fully into what they are feeling.)

Summary of the Technique

- The initiator feels triggered and says, "I would like to initiate, can you reflect?"
- The reflector says, "Yes I can."
- The initiator says, "I feel ___ because I think _____."
- The reflector says, "So let me see if I got this right. You feel _____ because you think _____. Is that right?"
- The initiator says yes or no, and the reflector finally says, "Is there more?"
- This continues for several sentences. Then after a pause to digest the information, if the reflector feels they have something that triggered them to feel a certain way, then that person can do some initiating in the same way.

Sample Sentences

- "I feel hurt because I think that you are rejecting me when you leave a conversation without telling me when you are coming back."

160

- "I feel angry because I think you deliberately don't take out the garbage to piss me off."
- "I feel sad because I think we are growing apart because we don't communicate often enough."

It is important that the sentence "I feel _____ because I think _____" be fundamentally respected; as the lead sentence, it is the most important sentence. The question "Is there more?" is also an important question. This is the goodwill question that allows the initiator the opportunity to *feel heard*. So often people do not feel heard, acknowledged or empathized with in fights or disagreements. The most healing aspect of the exercise is the reflector's hearing and acknowledging the other person. This is the most important indication that a person is not operating from the impulse of the hurt child, but from the balanced responsible adult. You may not agree with the other person, but you have given them the respect of taking in what they are saying and letting them know that they have been heard and acknowledged and their feelings metabolized. This is like medicine for a couple who has not been able to communicate properly. In my office, I hear people fretting that they will not get to a resolution or a solution with this technique. They question the value of simply initiating and reflecting. But I assure them that they can trust that this process is a proven and important sacred healing salve for a damaged relationship. And then, over time and with practice, they see the profound value of this technique. Sometimes the most crucial thing is not getting to a solution, but simply having the feelings heard. Acknowledging the other person's feelings and taking the time to listen carefully to what they are saying has a profoundly relaxing and healing impact on a relationship. Most often there is no way for one person to resolve the other person's feelings. Your feelings are your responsibility; it is not the other person's responsibility to solve your feelings. What is most important in a relationship is to make sure that each person is heard, respected and empathized with. You may not agree with each other, but at least you have built some goodwill and trust in the relationship with the knowledge that your feelings will be heard and acknowledged. This is a profound elixir for a troubled relationship.

After I encourage the initiator to ask three or four sentences so that they feel fully heard and acknowledged, I then encourage a pause. Then I ask the reflector if they would like to initiate. I ask that the person take a moment to see what they are feeling so that they can formulate a sentence and become the initiator as well. Remember that writing down your feelings before talking can be very helpful.

You're Either Contributing to the Mess or to the Cleanup in Your Relationship!

If you are in a disagreement, notice how much negativity you bring to a fight. Take personal responsibility for what you contribute to the moment of conflict. Refusing to stay in your adult, being impulsive, insulting the other person and refusing to engage in healthy techniques for fighting all contribute to the mess of the relationship. Conversely, staying in your adult, being patient, owning your responsibility in a fight and engaging in healthy techniques for conflict all contribute to the cleanup in the relationship.

Committing to using the Initiate-and-Reflect technique exclusively instead of fighting is an act of personal responsibility that says to the other person, "I am committed to the cleanup of this relationship and not to the mess." I encourage couples to practice this as soon as either one in the couple feels triggered, hurt, reactive and/or angry. They need to stick to the technique precisely so that they can get used to immediately defaulting into this technique as a way to manage triggers and conflicts. When people are not committed to the cleanup, they are contributing to the mess. This means that even though they are aware that old patterns of dysfunctional behavior are destroying the relationship, they are *choosing* to consciously continue to engage in the patterns of dysfunction. When a person is in their full adult self, they are cognizant that they have a choice and that they are not a victim. And when they have been shown a technique that works to ameliorate the dynamic, then a commitment to being a part of the cleanup is their responsibility.

The most important aspect of the Initiate-and-Reflect technique is that it prevents childish communication, defensiveness, impulsive rudeness and trying to make the other person responsible for one's feelings. It is an effective and proven way to build an atmosphere of trust and goodwill as opposed to descending into the land of reactivity and dysfunctional fighting. Building up the pot of goodwill in a relationship helps the relationship to weather through more difficult times. Any couple with whom I have worked who has diligently committed to this technique has managed to retreat significantly from intentions to divorce or separate. Their resentment levels go down profoundly, and the levels of trust that each feels toward the other improve significantly. They are able to behave like adults with one another, and they feel they are a team working together toward the common goal of having a peaceful yet passionate relationship-culture.

Variations on the Technique
Once a couple has mastered the initial very strict guidelines of the Initiate-and-Reflect exercise and has stuck to it for a number of months, I allow them to engage in the reflecting through the looser modality of "paraphrasing," which involves a person using different words to reflect what the speaker has said specifically. This shows not only that the

person is listening but also that they are attempting to deeply understand what the speaker is saying.

It is not uncommon for people to make assumptions and to judge, generalize and belittle what the other person is saying based on their own prejudices and opinions. Therefore, it is of paramount importance when paraphrasing the person to not bring in their own ideas or question the speaker's thoughts, feelings or actions. The paraphrasing responses need to honor the other person's words so that they are non-directive and non-judgmental. I often hear from couples that this technique can feel unnatural. We are trying to create a new normal in the communication that had previously been habituated in dysfunctionality and undisciplined repartee. Couples need to practice the technique of mirroring, reflecting and paraphrasing often so that this new normal can stand the test of time and create an atmosphere for the couple that is healthy, functional and emotionally safe. Practice, practice, practice in order to feel comfortable doing this.

Individual Work
Very often when I work with a couple with the hurt child and/or the above mentioned parent-child dynamic, there is a need to explore each of the couple's childhoods to understand the origins of the patterns. Individual work is sometimes needed so I can understand the inner workings and motivations for each person. After the individual work, they can come together to transform their relationship-culture from where it was — from dysfunctional relating to functional and healthy thriving as a couple.

You Cannot Change What You Are Not Aware Of
As I mentioned earlier, I encourage people to watch out for living in their false selves or the selves they created in response to family-culture dynamics in order to survive. One of the fundamental aspects of being in a successful

164

long-term relationship requires that both people get in touch with their innate authentic self-culture. This prevents the couple from going down the rabbit hole of denial and making decisions based on their lack of awareness. With the awareness gained from individual therapy, they are more apt to no longer use shame and guilt and the hurt child/parent dynamic as a go-to pattern of behavior. They understand the value of honoring the self and others. The hurt child no longer runs the show with helpless, passive or powerless behavior. I encourage both parties to do the work to step into their authentic adult selves so they can see life from the adult rather than the child perspective.

I recommend two exercises for each person in the couple to use so that they can develop and encourage their own unique self-culture, which will ultimately impact the relationship-culture in positive ways. Remember, awareness + willingness + courage = change. Once the three elements are in place, you can unearth the state of being of the "balanced adult voice." Once unearthed, by calling deeply upon it, this innate state of being cannot be altered. See appendix E "Exercise for Developing Your Self-Culture" and appendix F "Exercise for Anchoring Neural Pathways."

The Balanced Adult

Being in your balanced adult is most favorable for a healthy relationship-culture. It is through your balanced adult that you can have a balanced relationship-culture. How do you know when you are in your balanced adult? When the following elements are in place:

- You are non-judgmental.
- You allow others to be themselves.
- You are accepting of what is.
- You focus on and are oriented re the present day.

- You have trust and faith in the process of life.
- You deal with adversity by seeing the larger picture; you ask, "What is the lesson for me here?" (I call this "transcendence thinking.")
- You take responsibility for yourself in all aspects.
- You draw clear boundaries and stick to them.
- You commit to not enabling the hurt child or the critical parent in yourself or others.
- You are compassionate, yet not a caretaker.
- You encourage others to care for themselves.
- You quiet your mind often and listen to your own divine guidance.
- You honor yourself and listen to your own needs.
- You are authentic.
- You have focused, clear intentions in life.
- You have a positive, buoyant attitude.
- You're oriented toward action, not reaction.
- You believe that life is supportive.
- You are grateful.

Stepping into your empowered adult voice does not happen overnight. It is a process that evolves from a deep, repetitive practice of calling forward your balanced adult voice. The first steps begin with parenting yourself in compassionate ways. You begin to feel safe, which, in turn, encourages your authentic self to blossom. This is the way for the child to stop wanting to control and run the show.

The child is set free and gets to relax as the balanced adult steps up to manage the store. This is a golden process that allows us to move beyond the elements that limit our growth. It brings us into healthy relationships with other people and allows us the opportunity to step into our greatness and into our authentic self-culture.

Overfunctioning and Underfunctioning Patterns

It bears repeating that "overfunctioning" in a relationship creates a massive imbalance. In her book *Extraordinary Relationships: A New Way of Thinking about Human Interactions*, Roberta Gilbert defines a person as an overfunctioner when they are doing things for the other person that the other person is able to accomplish for themselves. They habitually give advice that is unsolicited and talk more than they listen. They feel responsible for their partner and often focus on goals that they think their partner should have, and they project this onto them. They often burn out because they too frequently take on more responsibility than they can handle. The overfunctioner finds solutions for their partner's problems, caretaking their emotions in a way that deprives them of the ability to take care of themselves. It's a fast way to destroy healthy dynamics in a relationship. Remember that when one person is overfunctioning, the other person will often underfunction, and their ability to function for themselves atrophies. The overfunctioner often becomes resentful because they feel obliged to do more than their share because the underfunctioner typically does way too little.

Overfunctioners need to stop enabling the underfunctioner. If you are an overfunctioner, it is important that you stop worrying about the other person's dreams, wants, goals, chores and life choices. Lean out of *them* and lean into *yourself*. Work on allowing each person to be responsible for their own emotional well-being and create a balanced division of chores in the home. This will safeguard the relationship by allowing each person to have healthy boundaries — saying yes only when you want to and allowing yourself to say no when you need to. I encourage couples to develop a dynamic in the relationship that includes a fair balance of energies. This includes divisions of labor that are fair and making sure everyone takes personal responsibility for their emotional well-being. The person who does too much of the functioning is often avoiding themselves by overfocusing on the other person. They need to ask themselves: "Why am I avoiding dealing with myself?" Usually there's something that may be too painful to look at, so it's easier to look at the other person instead. It's important to remember everyone is an adult in this relationship. Everyone needs to be responsible for themselves. If not, as I have seen repeatedly, toxicity inevitably starts to overtake the relationship.

There Is No Way Around the Mountain!

Understand that to truly resolve the pain, you need to go through the pain. It is the act of going through the pain that brings relief to the problem. Work on not escaping or numbing out what you feel by having an affair, drinking or some other escapist behavior. This will not help resolve the issues.

The only way to neutralize or minimize the pain is to look at the problem straight in the face and to go through it. There is no way around the mountain, you need to go through the mountain to get to the other side where there is light. You don't have to go through the mountain alone. You can find the tools and you can solicit advice and help from others to get through it.

Nevertheless, the journey does involve the arduous and sometimes painful task of going through a mountain as opposed to going around it. Understand that being addicted to comfort, numbing out and avoiding pain, only lead a person to escapist behavior that ultimately destroys a relationship. If you truly want to heal your relationship-culture, then I invite you to commit to going through some struggle and strife that can lead to healing and resolution.

Chapter 9

Fundamentals for Long-Term Passionate Relationships: Conscious Coupling

So now that you are both in your adult selves, the question is: What creates a successful long-term, passionate marriage/partnership?

John Gottman's "Love Lab"

Marriage researcher John Gottman did some foundational work studying couples by videotaping them and recording conversations to see whether happy and unhappy couples differed in any way. He put sensors on the couples and videotaped them as they talked about difficult marital topics. This was groundbreaking work in the 1970s.

The sensors revealed that the happiest couples were physiologically calm and relaxed, whereas the unhappiest couples were tense and ready to fight.[7] Gottman discovered the simple concept that the happiest marriages are based on deep friendship, a concept that later became the heart of his workshops and seminars, and that mutual respect and sincere enjoyment of each other's company is crucial to a good marriage.[8]

---

[7] John M. Gottman and Julie Schwartz Gottman, "The Empirical Basis of Gottman Couples Therapy," The Gottman Institute, 2013, https://www.gottman.com/wp-content/uploads/EmpiricalBasis-Update3.pdf.

[8] John M. Gottman and Nan Silver, *The Seven Principles for Making Marriage Work: A Practical Guide from the Country's Foremost Relationship Expert* (New York: Harmony Books, 2015), 20.

Making meticulous calculations, Gottman determined different mathematical patterns from his observations. He eventually developed what he would call the "Love Lab" at the University of Washington, where he could monitor couples' behavior in a home-like setting over many days. Gottman wanted to understand how couples successfully built intimacy and connection. He discovered that in coupledom, partners regularly put out bids for or attempts at connection, conversation or a response from each other. He discovered that the more often partners responded positively to the bids, the more they were able to build up a reservoir of positive emotions, which Gottman called the "Emotional Bank Account," that later benefited the couple when they encountered conflict. The research showed that being receptive to one another is the key to building positive connection and intimacy.[9]

Fix It Quickly!

An article in *Psychology Today* about John Gottman quotes him as saying, "Mostly, all you can do in love is repair how you screw up."[10] And quickly! Gottmann says that the best relationships are those in which partners work to repair actions and incidents that they feel bad about or regret. His "Threshold of Repair" metric shows that partners who own up to the damage they've done and immediately reach out to make amends keep minor damage from growing into an increasingly larger problem that swiftly compounds negatively. According to the article, he said that the most resilient of couples tend not to go down the road of profound negativity and that this made the connection more resilient against conflict.

---

[9] Ellie Lisitsa, "An Introduction to Emotional Bids and Trust," August 31, 2012, http://www.gottmanblog.com/archives/2014/10/28/an-introduction-to-emotional-bids-and-trust.

[10] Kristin Ohlson, "The Einstein of Love," *Psychology Today* (October 2015),74.

Good Sex — Often!

The one thing that always stands out as sustaining the longevity of a relationship and a strong relationship-culture is good chemistry; that is, good sex! The positive nesting effects that the biochemistry of intimacy creates is profoundly important to create goodwill, interest in one another, passion, sexiness and flirtation. Of course, if a relationship has all kinds of other elements that make them compatible, such as good communication and mutual hobbies, good sex is going to factor in less, but it is still important. And conversely, if they are incompatible in other areas, sex is going to be even more important to the longevity of a couple's relationship. Sex is an amazing bridge that can rekindle connectedness and closeness when day-to-day life takes over, resulting in fatigue and creating distance between them.

Research suggests that in long-term committed relationships, passion and sex can wane over time; however, many couples do manage to maintain the passion. Research suggests that sexual dissatisfaction has been closely linked to greater incidences of conflict as well as unhappiness and instability in the marriage.[11,12]

The question is, how do some long-term committed married couples manage to maintain their sexual connection? A possible key to this question is found in a concept called "communal strength," which refers to a general inclination to fulfill the needs of your partner

---

[11] Pew Research Center, "Modern Marriage," July 18, 2007, http://www.pewsocialtrends.org/2007/07/18/modern-marriage.

[12] Thomas D. Williams, "Sexless Marriage in America Keeps Rising, New Study Reveals," *Breitbart*, January 2, 2015, http://www.breitbart.com/big-government/2015/01/02/sexless-marriage-in-america-keeps-rising-new-study-reveals.

without the need to keep score, thus building resentment.[13] Amy Muise, a postdoctoral fellow in psychology at the University of Toronto Mississauga, sought to understand how the concept of communal strength applies to sexuality in long-term couples. Her studies concluded that couples who were more communal had a better sexual connection; that is, partners who were more inclined to have sex when their partner wanted to have sex tended to maintain the sexual connection for the long haul.[14] This was not to say that the marriage was Victorian-style, in which spousal obligations dominated the scenario. Not at all! Instead, as Muise says in the *Psychology Today* article, "It's not that they were begrudgingly doing it when they didn't want to, they were motivated to meet their partner's needs and felt good about doing that. They also felt more satisfied with their relationship, and their partner did too."[15]

When I see couples who have very different sexual appetites, I recommend that the partner who is less sexually inclined try to have sex more often anyway when their partner approaches them, and every time I hear that even though they were not in the mood, once they started to get into it, they enjoyed themselves. To be clear, this is not about codependent self-sacrifice. This is about an adult conscious decision to participate in supporting the very matrix that keeps the relationship strong and alive, which includes participating in sex often.

---

[13] Susan Krauss Whitbourne, "How the Best Couples Keep Their Romantic Spark Alive," *Psychology Today*, August 27, 2013, https://www.psychologytoday.com/blog/fulfillment-any-age/201308/how-the-best-couples-keep-their-romantic-spark-alive.
[14] Amy Muise, Emily A. Impett, and Serge Desmarais, "Getting It On versus Getting It Over With: Sexual Motivation, Desire, and Satisfaction in Intimate Bonds," *Personality and Social Psychology Bulletin* (June 28, 2013): 3, doi: 10.1177/0146167213490963.
[15] Jennifer Bleyer. "Good in Bed," *Psychology Today* 48, no. 5 (2015): 42–43.

Sex is definitely a use-it-or-lose-it prospect! Neural pathways associated with sexuality are strengthened and maintained if sex is engaged in often. The neural pathways associated with sex will weaken if frequently left on the back burner. Making sure that those neural pathways are kept alive, well and healthy is crucial for a strong and healthy relationship-culture. Strong neural pathways associated with sexuality keep the desire for one another alive and well. Daily sexual expressions, such as touching each other in sexy ways, especially outside of the bedroom, as well as kissing, hugging, cuddling and flirting all go a long way toward keeping alive the neural pathways that are associated with sexuality and lovemaking. These expressions of sexuality need to occur many times during the week, preferably daily. Also, lovemaking at least once or twice a week is ideal to keep the neural pathways alive for the long haul. Remembering that there are many kinds of sexual encounters to be explored is important as well.

There are the quickies, the long drawn-out sessions, the everything-but-intercourse sessions, the sexy shower-time sessions and more. This all contributes significantly to a couple's being interested in one another and feeling a deep attraction for and excitement about one another. These are important fundamental keys to sustain a long-term, passionate relationship-culture.

It always concerns me when I hear a couple say they no longer have sex very often. If a couple cannot find their way back to having regular sex, I am often doubtful that the couple will survive. No matter how busy a couple may find themselves, they need to find time for sex. They need to prioritize it, schedule it in and make it central to their relationship. Thinking about each other when apart, sending sexy text messages, talking about sex when outside of the bedroom, flirting and sexy touch are all ways to contribute to feeling hot for one another. This is a wonderfully strong motivating factor in keeping a couple connected and together. The oxytocin released when we have good, intimate, connected sex goes a long way toward keeping the nesting intentions alive and well for both people. I am convinced that it is possible to maintain this for the long haul, especially when both parties are able to stay in their adult selves. When we are in our adult selves, we are less likely to be impulsive and more likely to handle boredom in a healthy way by creating special moments with one another, day in and day out.

Regular Touch

Regular touch that doesn't lead to sex also feeds the biochemistry of connection between the couple. I ask couples to hug each other regularly, kiss, hold hands, cuddle and even slow dance affectionately in the living room during the day in a spare moment or after everyone else has gone to bed. When couples have children, they often deposit all of their touch onto their children, or their pets, as if they are the only ones who need regular and constant affection. In reality, constant and regular touch and affection are like a deposit into the couple's connection-and-passion bank account that needs to be made daily to keep the account healthy and full. I often see couples who have been together for a while almost ignore each other and take each other for granted because they don't realize the importance of touch and affection on the human experience. They stopped treasuring the human being with whom they chose to be in a long-term committed relationship. And then they wondered why they felt bored and the relationship no longer felt special. They had simply stopped depositing energy into the other person, or, as a way to punish them, they had allowed unresolved resentment to build up, which led to the other person's being deprived of much-needed affection.

Be a Cheerleader

In reality, it is hard to be fully attracted to someone if you do not feel emotionally safe, free and comfortable with them. If you harbor resentment for your partner, it is difficult to be hot for that person, especially if you are in a long-term relationship or marriage. Therefore, it is particularly important for the health of the relationship and for each person in the relationship to believe that the other person is their cheerleader and their biggest supporter. When each person knows that, no matter what, their partner has their back and will make every effort to not be judgmental or critical, it has a profoundly healing and bonding effect on the couple and on the relationship-culture. It is deeply connecting and relaxing when both people in the couple know that they will never be publicly humiliated, shamed or cruelly mocked by the other person. Each person needs to be able to completely trust that their emotions, feelings and reputation are safe with their partner. Each person also needs to know that the other person feels compassion and goodwill toward them. This creates a beautiful bond. They know that they can feel confident that their partner will stand up for them and that they will be supported and loved, flaws and all. This is the ideal relationship-culture that truly beautiful, long-term, passionate relationships emanate from.

Mutual Interests

It is important for a couple to have mutual interests. I'm not saying you have to love the same things. But you need to have a few things that you like to do together. You both like to hang out on a beach or at a park. You both like to play tennis. You both like to ski, or you both enjoy pets or politics, cooking, dining, walking or some other interest. However, Gottman cautions couples, when they do engage in activities together, that they not use that platform as an excuse for criticism and overcontrolling. "Do it this way!" "You need to keep your eye on the ball!"[16] Such behavior will surely deplete the pot of goodwill that could then harm the relationship-culture. It is important when couples engage in activities together that they do so in a fun, emotionally safe and caring way so as to continually build a deeper affection for and friendship with one another.

I think it is also healthy for couples to have their own separate interests. As I mentioned in chapter 2, it is attractive for people have their own passions. Each person needs to have an independent, self-satisfying life, but they often come together to share in an interest and in intimacy. Being overly intertwined and enmeshed never works well for the healthiness of the relationship-culture. Yet being overly independent also does not bode well for a healthy relationship-culture. A healthy balance needs to be struck so that the relationship-culture can draw from the independent time as well as the shared time. I observe this to be the best model for a couple to sustain longevity and passion in their relationship-culture.

Minimize Jealousy and Envy

It is important to minimize jealousy and envy, especially when there is no evidence or foundation based on the other person's behavior. This is fundamental for a successful and healthy relationship-culture. If your partner is not a flirt or does not take mysterious time away from you, please do not worsen the situation with absurd, unfounded jealousy.

Instead, fortify your relationship-culture with mutual trust, being happy for the other person and honoring each other's boundaries. Jealousy is often about one's insecurity and

---

[16] Gottman and Silver, *The Seven Principles*, 14.

lack of self-esteem and self-care, which the jealous partner projects onto the other person. The foundation of jealousy is a feeling of emptiness and expecting the other person to fill the void they feel inside themselves. I encourage each person to consistently work on their self-care, filling their own cup first so that they feel full and self-confident and giving to the other only from the overflow.

With regard to envy, if your partner is professionally successful, and you are struggling with your own success, I encourage you to find it within yourself to be happy for your partner because, more often than not, to be happy and joyous about your partner's success will, on many energetic levels, open up success for you.

Be Transparent

I encourage couples to always be transparent with each other. It is vital that each person in the couple be sincere and honest with the other person. This builds mutual trust. Tell each other your passwords for all your electronic devices and bank accounts and always make truth a foundational element in the relationship. Secrecy and hiding are the domain of dysfunction and toxicity.

Loyalty, Trust and Accountability

Each person in the couple needs to know that their partner is always going to be loyal and trustworthy and accountable to them. Small lies, small deceptions, even white lies all contribute to the toxicity and demise of the relationship. Being inauthentic or operating from the false self is part of the destruction of loyalty, trust and accountability. The energy within the couple needs to be that of full relaxation with and trust in one another. That doesn't mean that you don't make an effort for the other person or just let yourself go. No! That means that both people feel a profound trust that the other person will always be loyal to them. Accountability means that both people regularly let each other know where they are at emotionally and physically. Accountability means that you don't leave the other person in the dark regarding your physical location or how you feel emotionally. Accountability also means that you talk about how you spend your money and what your priorities are regarding your finances. Honesty, truth, authenticity, loyalty, accountability and trust are all the domain of a healthy relationship-culture.

Prioritize Appropriately

When I work with couples who are having trouble, I often begin our work by asking them to prioritize a list of items that I give them. The list includes self, partner, children, family/parents, work and friends. Usually each person puts their children first, then work, then family/parents, then partner, then friends and then self. In my opinion, this is why the relationship is in trouble. Their priorities are not beneficial to a healthy relationship-culture. As I have said many times, I believe the self needs to be first — you need to fill your own cup first, create a deep vitality within and then give to others only from the overflow. This is the only way to keep from operating from resentment. If the self is empty, then that person is likely to project that emptiness onto their partner, and this leads to dysfunction, toxicity and problems. So the self should be number one; however, a very close second, number one A, needs to be the couple! I repeat, the couple needs to be a very close second in the list of priorities because, if the self and the couple are doing well, then the children will do well and the family will do well and even the job will do well, as will the friendships. But if the self and the couple are not doing well, everything will fall apart.

Respectful Communication

"Familiarity breeds contempt" is an adage that needs to be watched out for. When couples come to see me for relationship counseling, one of the first rules that I quickly impose in the office is that the communication needs to be respectful and kind, even when they bring up areas of contention or conflict. People can be direct and forthright; however, when couples normalize disrespectful and careless communication, the bridge to healing and getting back to intimacy is a long and difficult road, if reached at all. I find that for long-term passionate relationships to exist, it is important for couples to adhere to the concept of "careful communication" from the get-go; in other words, "mindful communication." I believe that the foundation of a relationship's communication needs to be careful, kind and considerate, and when transgressions do occur, as is bound to happen, both people need to understand that they need to apologize as soon as they realize that they have been rude, hurtful or disrespectful. We are all responsible for our speech and how we communicate. We have a right to express our anger, but we need to do it in responsible ways. Over time, when a couple is no longer careful about how they speak to one another, the relationship erodes. Attrition occurs when people are disrespectful, passive-aggressive, mocking or humiliating. However, no one is perfect; therefore, apologizing and owning up when one makes mistakes goes a long way toward creating emotional safety, compassion and goodwill between the couple.

Good communication includes lots of mirroring, empathy, compassion, validation and support, especially when the communication involves revealing tender truths. It is always heartening to know that your partner will validate the courage it took for you to reveal something deep and precious. Honoring each other's process is also part of good and respectful communication. Watch out for giving unsolicited advice. It is never going to be well received! Also know that you cannot save the other person. Allow the other person to work out their own issues. Practice the good habit of listening when the other person speaks and valuing each other's words and truths with a generous spirit.

Having said all this, fights do happen, and sometimes they get ugly, but what needs to be remembered is what Gottman says in his book *Seven Principles for Making Marriage Work*: "After intensely studying happily married couples for as long as sixteen years, I now know that the key to reviving or divorce-proofing a relationship is not in how you handle disagreements but in how you are with each other when you're not fighting. So although my Seven Principles will also guide you in coping with conflict, the foundation of my approach is to strengthen the friendship that is at the heart of any marriage."[17]

Noticing, Paying Attention, Performing Goodwill Deeds

A good relationship-culture is one that includes couples noticing and paying attention to each other in small ways. Goodwill deeds and random acts of kindness are like a healing elixir for a couple who wants a long-term and passionate relationship-culture. I'm not saying every interaction needs to be lovey-dovey or effusive because that wouldn't be natural or possible. However, listening, paying attention and verbally acknowledging each other are often massively important tools that create emotional closeness, safety and intimacy. I encourage couples to look into each other's eyes when they are speaking, especially if the topic includes deeper vulnerable content. Say "I love you" often. Find ways to positively reinforce the other person, noticing when they do something that is nice or sweet. Look to

---

[17] Ibid., 46.

uplift your partner instead of criticize them. Look for the positive traits versus the flaws. Everyone has flaws, and the ideal experience is to have your partner love you unconditionally despite your flaws and for you to do the same for your partner. Remember the times when you were dating and bring that energy into your relationship, whether you've been together for one year, ten years or more. Also remember that what you focus on expands. If you focus too much on the negative, the negative will expand, so make the effort to focus in on the positive often. I invite you to find daily opportunities to positively reinforce and cheerlead your partner.

Get in the Present Moment

I understand that people can become bored in long-term relationships. But if both people in the relationship get fully into the present moment, treasuring the here and now and the magnificence therein, they will find the sure-fire answer to boredom. Remember that being an adult means not giving into impulsiveness to relieve boredom. Being an adult means staying in the moment and valuing the moment you are in, and the person who is in the moment with you needs to be valued as important and special as well. For long-term passionate relationships to occur, an effort needs to be made to make sure that each and every moment is seen and treasured.

"Get present!" Start seeing the present moment as the most precious thing you could possibly have. When you do this, you will see one of two things: (1) You will start to profoundly value what is in front of you, or (2) you will start to see what is actually there but that you have been ignoring. If what is in front of you is not working, your deeply present self will make you aware of what you need to do to really change your situation. Honoring and living profoundly in the present moment is the antidote to all boredom and all denial.

I invite all people who are in committed, long-term relationships to start today to notice how often they are in the present and how often they are not. Listen to your inner voice. Listen to your partner. Pay attention to the small things. I invite you get into the present moment every single day; wake up, be present and notice this partner, this moment, this experience and this life that is yours!

Reveal Your Vulnerable Side

In her book *Daring Greatly*, Brené Brown, a favorite author of mine, writes, "Rather than ... hurling judgement and advice, we must dare to show and let ourselves be seen. This is vulnerability,"[18] and "If we can share our story with someone who responds with empathy and understanding, shame can't survive,"[19] and "Vulnerability is the core, the heart, the center, of meaningful human experiences."[20]

Vulnerability can augment intimacy, safety and emotional healing between two people. It is a fundamental way to bridge communication, reduce shame and enrich a partnership. Many people are not in touch with their vulnerability because they are too accustomed to building protective walls that mask it. They probably learned this in their family-culture, where to survive they needed to build walls instead of allow their vulnerable side to come forth. In reality, when a person is triggered, they may react with anger, irritability, annoyance and frustration, which, when

---

[18] Brené Brown, *Daring Greatly: How the Courage to Be Vulnerable Transforms the Way We Live, Love, Parent, and Lead* (New York: Gotham Books, 2012), 2.
[19] Ibid., 75.
[20] Ibid., 12.

peeled back, we discover that what is lying underneath is hurt, sadness, pain, abandonment and/or feelings of rejection. When people can come to the table, after peeling away their armor — their protective outer shield — with a truth that is authentically vulnerable, they are much more likely to be well received by their partner. When revealing the more vulnerable side of yourself, you are saying, "I am not perfect and neither are you, and that's okay; we can work on this together." When this energy is present within a couples' therapy session, we have something to work with that can promote healing and transformation in a couple. When a person starts to communicate with their partner on the level of vulnerability, a powerful alchemy of change occurs.

If you are in a discussion with your partner and find yourself defensive, irritable or annoyed, know that if you choose to sit with yourself quietly and pay attention to your inner thoughts, you will allow your real feelings to surface, which inevitably will be more vulnerable feelings that will be less damaging to the dynamic. Once you are in touch with those feelings, I encourage you to come the discussion with that instead.

Pay attention to your vulnerable truth that is underneath a big layer of armor — seeming truth that isn't actual truth, but rather a protective coating that just creates separation and breaks the bridge of intimacy and communication.

Emotional Self-Sufficiency

Taking responsibility for one's own happiness is a key component to a healthy, stable and passionate relationship-culture. This is an ideal environment to nurture a healthy and passionate relationship-culture. Couples who are emotionally overly enmeshed become codependent, which leads to toxic dysfunction. Being in one's adult aspect means that everyone is taking personal responsibility for what is happening emotionally to themselves. An example of a completely unhealthy and destructive interaction is when one person who may be feeling emotionally empty then projects all of that emptiness onto the other person, essentially demanding that the other person fill their emptiness. I find that couples are much more interested and attracted to each other when both people are willing to take responsibility for their bouts of emotional emptiness as well as their flaws and foibles. This kind of adult action goes a long way toward creating a fantastic matrix of healthy connection for the couple.

Humor

A study that examined the effects of humor on relationships in pleasant versus conflict situations found that individuals who were more satisfied with their romantic relationships reported using higher levels of positive humor and lower levels of negative humor than those individuals who were less satisfied in their romantic relationships.[21] The study also found that individuals who were not satisfied with their romantic relationships did not reduce their use of negative humor, which suggests that they did not use strategies to de-escalate a conflict. Couples who were in happy relationships tended to use less negative humor as a way to de-escalate a conflict situation. The authors of this study interpreted this shift in humor use as part of a strategy that is used by those with high relationship satisfaction to avoid further escalation of conflict with their romantic partners. Basically, the less you happen to value your relationship, the less you will preserve it by being

---

[21] Bethany Butzer and Nicholas A. Kuiper, "Humor Use in Romantic Relationships: The Effects of Relationship Satisfaction and Pleasant versus Conflict Situations," *The Journal of Psychology* 142, no. 3 (2008): 245–260.

unmindful about what would make something worse or better. Using negative humor is associated with lower levels of relationship satisfaction, whereas greater conflict resolution is associated with higher levels of satisfaction. In a positive relationship-culture, people are responsible for how they use humor. Sarcasm, passive aggressiveness and digs are all part of negative humor and work to tear down a relationship. Using positive humor to uplift your partner and to lighten and encourage the energy of the couple is a good strategy to maintain relationship-culture satisfaction.

Love Languages

I often recommend Gary Chapman's book *The 5 Love Languages: The Secret to Love That Lasts* when I work with couples. He brilliantly outlines different expressions of love that people may gravitate toward due to their personalities. He has a wonderful test that I often give out in the office so that couples can understand what their love language is. He asks the question, "What if you could say or do just the right thing to make that special someone feel loved?" So many couples in my practice say, "I just don't feel as though he loves me," and the other person says, "I tried to do everything for her, and I don't feel appreciated." People experience love in different ways, and it is important to find out what your partner needs to feel loved.

In *The 5 Love Languages*, Chapman refers to words of affirmation, quality time, receiving gifts, acts of service and physical touch as the five languages of love. If someone experiences love through words of affirmation, yet their partner wants physical touch as their language of love, then there is going to be a mismatch. To find the common ground is the alchemy that is needed to heal the miscommunications that may occur in expressions of love, people need to understand what their love language is and gently let their partner know what that is so that there is a greater chance for a positive connection to occur. Dr. Chapman has posted his test widely on the internet, and I encourage couples to do the five love-languages test to accurately determine which love language best suits each person. They can then share this information with each other so as to create a bridge for communication and for connection. This kind of thing does wonders for rewiring a relationship-culture that engages in habits that do not help the relationship. When we know what one another's love language is, we can incorporate that into the way we relate to one another.

Lean Out

I want to speak about a technique that I recommend often when I notice that one of the people in a couple is in a constant state of anxiety and preoccupation with the other person. This can look like control, excessive worry and jealousy. The person is not looking at themselves and their own life enough. They are perhaps in an avoidance that is fueled by a feeling of emptiness or imbalance in their own life, and to cope and fill the void, they look to the other person to fill that emptiness, and they overly fixate on the other person. When anxiety shows up, people tend to be overly controlling and place obsessive attention on perfectionism and detail. They tend to lean in and obsessively try to fix what they perceive is wrong. They think they need to have control to feel safe. Feeling anxious activates the fight-or-flight response, and people begin to panic; they leap into survival mode and become hypervigilant, which leads to leaning in to the other person, which, in turn, falsely and temporarily makes them feel safer. When people lean in, they make poor choices.

An important tool to cope with anxiety is to "lean out." Leaning out of the other person and leaning into your *self* is what I'm speaking about. Instead of avoiding, I invite you to go in and do a self-exploration so that you may look at whatever imbalance or emptiness may be inside you. Look the monster in the eye and find out what it is trying to teach *you* about *you*. When leaning out of the other person, you engage in the energy of surrender. You send a message to the Universe that you feel trust and, in turn, a similar mirroring energy of trust comes back to you. You enter an energy of allowing, not controlling. You send a message that you trust in life. The neural pathways of anxiety are then interrupted because you choose to consistently stop the thoughts that caused the panic. A new normal ensues.

Case Study: What Does Leaning Out Look Like?

Rachel and Daryl had been together eight years. They had been married for four of those years and had two beautiful little children. Over the years, a pattern had evolved whereby Rachel would consistently worry about Daryl's habit of withdrawing into himself. He had unresolved depression, shutting Rachel out, as well as their children.

He would often avoid participation in the relationship for long periods. He was doing the best he could with his mental state, and besides spending long hours at the office, he would sometimes muster the energy to socialize with his male friends. However, he didn't seek out therapy, and this made Rachel feel anxious and jealous of any time he spent outside of the home with other people.

No matter what she said to him, he refused to change. She tried to control him, berating him and pleading with him to talk. None of this got her what she desired, which was for him to care for his mental health and to once again feel the connection between them. However, none of her tactics made her feel that she was a priority to him. When she came in to see me and told me of her situation, I had to let her know that all the worry and all the control in the world was not going to force him to do what she wanted him to do. It was his choice if he was going to get help. She needed to lean out of him and lean back into herself. When I gave her this suggestion, a look of despair came over her face. She told me that nothing would ever change if she didn't take control of everything — in effect, be an overfunctioner. I asked her if what she had been doing was working for her. She said no. I told her to try something different. Even though this would cause immense fear, she was willing to give it a try since what she was doing was not working at all. She started to discipline herself to not be as overly involved with her partner's comings and goings as she had been. She also stopped asking what he was doing about his mental health. She started to realize this was his responsibility, and he needed to choose to seek out therapy and take care of his mental wellness, not her.

She was leaning out. She found other activities to curb the impulse to control her partner. She stopped texting him five times a day. She had been depending on him to drive her everywhere because she didn't know how to drive. She since learned how to drive. She took control of her own life and leaned out of his. The question was, would the relationship survive when her overfunctioning ceased to be the mainstay of the relationship?

What transpired was quite remarkable. Her partner began to seek her out more. He was now leaning into her because of the void that she had created when she stopped leaning into him. He made an appointment with a therapist and started to get some help. Nature abhors a void; the void will be filled with something if you allow the void to be there in the first place. Control and overfunctioning are the domain of a toxic relationship-culture. Letting go and allowing people to take responsibility for themselves is a healthy relationship-culture.

Part VI
Divorce

"Why do people leave?... People leave because they stop trying and because they have no idea how to break cycles of dysfunction and patterns of behavior that they may have learned from their family-culture. There's an old adage that says that doing the same thing over and over and expecting a different result is the definition of madness. When people come in to see me for couples' counseling, I have observed them doing the same thing they have been doing for too long, and although it isn't working, they just can't seem to stop their patterns of behavior..."
- **Victoria Lorient-Faibish**

Chapter 10
Why Does It Sometimes Go Wrong?

Listen, I understand; marriage is hard. It is a lot of hard work. It can be an uphill battle. I tell people who enter my office for marriage counseling that the journey may not be easy, but it is worth it. Some of what I talk about in this chapter may make some of you feel uncomfortable, but I believe it is worth being honest to help prevent the demise of relationships, which, with work and effort, could survive and even thrive.

Let me be clear that I am not talking about abusive (physical or otherwise), toxic relationships that involve deliberately malicious and devious behavior. I am also not talking about relationships that have one or both people involved in morbid addictions. These types of relationships are profoundly destructive and need to be broken up as soon as possible. They are toxic, and oftentimes people become addicted to the roller-coaster ride of toxicity, and they stay together long after their past due date.

In this chapter I discuss relationships that have promise but have gone bad due to a lack of tools to communicate and a lack of emotional discipline.

Why do people leave? I believe there is no way around the mountain on this one. People leave because they stop trying and because they have no idea how to break cycles of dysfunction and patterns of behavior that they may have learned from their family-culture. There's an old adage that says that doing the same thing over and over and expecting a different result is the definition of madness. When people come in to see me for couples' counseling, I have observed them doing the same thing they have been doing for too long, and although it isn't working, they just can't seem to stop their patterns of behavior.

A common thread I observe when people break up after they have been together a while is that they met before they knew themselves fully, and they chose a partner based on a false self that they had constructed as a way to deal with and survive the family-culture they came from. However, this false self, brought about through childhood experience, now no longer jibes with the person's adult life. Tastes, wants and habits that were survival tools during childhood now begin to clash with their adult lives. I have a witnessed people's false selves lead, later on in life, to nervous breakdowns, breakups, cheating, addiction, depression and anxiety.

As people find their authentic selves later on in life, they realize that the person they chose to marry and construct a family with no longer fits who they have become in their true self-culture.

Case Study
Mary and John were high school sweethearts. They lived in a small town and fell deeply in love when they were sixteen. They had many friends and were the popular, good-looking couple of the school. They were slated for success in all ways. The community around them cheered them on and supported their every move toward deeper and deeper commitment. Mary came from a deeply dysfunctional home in which her father was narcissistic and her mother was a compliant caretaker who encouraged the kids to kowtow to their dad's moods and rages. They were

192

ordered to toe the line, fly under the radar and simply obey whatever they were told. Mary's needs were low on the totem pole of priorities in her family-culture. She grew up as the eldest daughter of four, knowing that she had to put all her own needs aside. She cared for her younger siblings since her mother was too ensconced in trying to please her dad and maintain a full-time job. Her mother also battled depression and a gambling addiction.

Mary found solace in her relationship with John, who was a very social boy, and she loved being with him because she didn't have to think about her family as the two of them engaged in a lot of drugs, drinking and partying. Mary didn't want to feel her emotions, and the kind of connection she had with John allowed her to assuage some of the deep sadness she felt due to her family-culture issues. Partying was a staple in their social lives.

Eventually, they both graduated from high school and went to different post-secondary schools. She studied to become a teacher and he, a business administrator. There were long periods when they didn't see each other, and when they did, the passion was explosive — and so was the drinking. Mary laughed when she told me they were both functional addicts. They loved their wine, and they developed a love of pairing good wine with food. This became their routine over the next few years. They eventually got married and had two children. As the rearing of the children ensued, Mary was unable to keep up with the alcohol consumption, but John continued in the same way.

As Mary drank less, she started to feel her emotions more — and this was when she ended up in therapy with me. As she began to discover what her true self-culture was, she began to discover that she had a lot of feelings to process and resolve from her childhood. She started to realize that she needed to have a greater connection with John. She would reach out to him but was unable to create that connection. They were in very different places. She also decided that she wanted to join a 12-step program to help her with her drinking. John categorically thought that Mary was absolutely ridiculous in this pursuit. As her therapy evolved, and her self-exploration unfolded, John and Mary became increasingly more distant.

The person Mary was becoming was not at all the person she was when she had met John. As she evolved, she pleaded with John that he evolve alongside her. But he was not at all willing to stop drinking, and, in addition, he felt he didn't need to engage in therapy. He said to Mary, "Therapy is for you, not me. I'm fine. You're the one with the problems." The stance that John took started to build immense walls of resentment between them. Any tools that Mary learned in therapy were of no interest to John.

And we discovered the foundation of closeness and passion they had thought was once there was actually inauthentic. Alcohol was the emotional lubricant that kept them going. And when alcohol was no longer there, the closeness started to dissolve. Compounding this, John was not willing to support Mary emotionally on her journey. He took on a mocking tone that deeply hurt Mary and reminded her of her childhood and how her father had treated her. The walls of resentment grew, and, sadly, since John was not willing to engage in couples' therapy, they eventually did divorce.

Why Do People Cheat?

Of course, there is not one answer to the question "why do people cheat?" I can only tell you from what I have observed in my office over the 20 years that I've been doing work on relationships that people often seek sexual and emotional attention outside the relationship largely because they are not getting what they need within the relationship. This is not to say that this is the correct way to act. In fact, it is an unhealthy way to act and completely lacks integrity. When people find themselves dissatisfied, instead of living a double life that is full of lies, I invite them to either take their leave from the relationship if they have no other way to salvage the connection, or, before they go and have an affair, to deeply mine their own issues with personal self-esteem, boredom, impulsiveness and living in the hurt child aspect of themselves.

It is fully the responsibility of each person to get what they need from themselves. However, being in a long-term committed relationship requires a tremendous amount of effort to maintain the connection between the two people so that, in addition to getting what they need from themselves, they also get what they need from the relationship. For example, I strongly caution people about having emotional affairs at work. Even though many people have said to me that they think this is a harmless way to get their emotional needs met, I quickly let them know this will certainly lead to physical infidelity, even if they've promised themselves this would not occur. I remind folks that drinking alcohol lowers the person's resolve and willpower to maintain their commitments to themselves. For example, two people who have an emotional relationship at work suddenly, after a couple of drinks at an after-work event, find themselves tipsy, a state in which all discipline and resolve go out the window, and they fall into the choice of crossing the line of their emotional affair into a physical affair. It is a slippery slope that people need to be very, very careful with.

Case Study
Fanny found herself completely turned off by her husband and the way he made love to her, including how he touched her and how he courted her during foreplay. By the time

195

she came in to see me as a client, the sexual relationship was nearly null and void. They had been together for eight years, and it struck me when she said they were amazing partners and friends but terrible lovers. They loved to tend to their immense garden together, and they enjoyed weekly outings to take care of the horse they owned jointly.

Yet sexually they just did not mesh. She said it had been like this from the get-go. She thought things would improve as time went on, but they never did, and so they settled into a basically sexless marriage with brief moments of sexuality when they went on vacation once a year. Fanny's self-esteem was not very high when they had started dating, and so instead of waiting for the right partner, she decided to accept Edward's marriage proposal because she thought he was the best she could get. However, as Fanny's personal work in therapy deepened, her self-esteem, self-love and self-care increased. She started to engage in exercise, healthy eating and meditation. This helped her to like herself more, physically and emotionally. For the first time she felt strong and confident and pretty.

They didn't have any children and didn't plan to have any, and even though she contemplated leaving her husband, the courage to do so was just not there. She felt afraid of being alone in her old age, and she didn't want to hurt him.

It is my philosophy that *when you are unwilling or unable to change your life circumstance, you need to change yourself so that you can accept what is in your life*. I asked Fanny to work on making profound efforts with her husband in the realms of sexuality, flirting and connection. I asked her to carve out time with him and to schedule sex more often so that they could develop and grow in that realm. I even suggested that they see a sex therapist. They needed to establish new memories with positive sexual experiences therein. She did make valiant attempts to communicate honestly with her husband about the way he made love and about the way he connected with her sexually. She wanted him to initiate more; however, this never came to fruition. Nothing seemed to significantly change the dynamic. From my observation, it looked as though they were just badly matched sexually. To be blunt, there was no chemistry. They were turned on by different things and different atmospheres.

And even though they were great friends, it seemed to me that the changes that were required to improve their relationship were unlikely to materialize. Edward also refused to come in for therapy. With her unsuccessful efforts, Fanny mourned the fact that even though she was a very sexual person and longed to have good, compatible and satisfying sex, this might never happen with her husband. Yet she was unwilling to leave her marriage. Her realizations about her sexual needs did not wane either.

Fanny gave in to something that definitely was against her moral code. She began having a sexual and emotional affair with a co-worker at her office. The connection started quite innocently but quickly evolved into an intense physical and emotional connection. Her double life began to cause her extreme anxiety. When I asked her why she didn't leave her husband instead of lying to him, she said that she could not bear the thought of hurting him, and she really did not want to be alone. She had the idea that they would grow old together, and since they were such good friends, she thought this would work out well because she was certain that her sexual libido would decrease over time. This was a classic case of wanting her cake and eating it too, which is something that emanates from the child self. The adult confronts life head on and makes the difficult yet responsible choices. The child refuses to take the personal responsibility of making difficult choices. I let her know that it would be much kinder and in the spirit of true friendship to tell her husband the truth. I said that she was really doing him a disservice by lying to him. He had a right to know what the real state of his marriage was. He also had the right to seek out a partner who was a better match for him rather than be lied to.

Inevitably, when people live this double life and continually lie, the shame and guilt begin to take over and their self-esteem descends profoundly. Their value systems and their self-value go out the window. This then becomes a perpetuating cycle of dysfunction and self-destruction.

Eventually, Fanny was found out by Edward, who had started to become suspicious. A series of texts that Fanny had neglected to delete became the proof that Edward needed to confirm his suspicions. They did try to do some couples' work to salvage the marriage, but, alas, the damage of the lies was too deep and the marriage broke up.

Porn and Its Impact on Relationships

The use of porn today has become ubiquitous due to its easy availability. People no longer have to go out of their way to watch porn or go into some embarrassing sex shop to consume sexual material. Today it can happen with a simple click of a mouse right in your own home, and it can happen as often as a person wants! And although I am not a prude about nudity or sexuality, and I don't place any value judgment on people who enjoy watching porn, I feel it is my duty to talk about how porn impacts committed relationships. In a study[1] of men and women, ages eighteen

---

[1] Amanda M. Maddox, Galena K. Rhoades, and Howard J. Markman, "Viewing Sexually Explicit Materials Alone or Together: Associations

to thirty-four, all in romantic relationships, researchers measured the levels of negative communication, relationship adjustment, dedication or interpersonal commitment, sexual satisfaction and infidelity and found that 76.8% of men and 34.6% of women looked at sexually explicit material alone; 44.8% reported viewing it with partners. They found that people who didn't view *any* porn had *lower* levels of negative communication, were more committed to the relationship, and had higher sexual satisfaction and relationship adjustment. Their rate of infidelity was *at least half* of those who had watched sexual material alone *and* with their partners.

But people who watched porn only with their partners were more dedicated to the relationship and more sexually satisfied than those who watched alone.

The researchers also discovered that watching porn reminds people of all the potential sexual partners out there, which then lowers their allegiance to the person they are *in a relationship with*. It also leads people to switching out the person who's actually in bed with them in favor of the flight-of-the-imagination person they have never met and probably never will meet. This study seems to show that porn exposure does lead to real-world infidelity, and thus is not as harmless as one might think, especially when it comes to long-term committed relationships.

Sexless Marriages

In the many years of doing this work, I have observed that couples who have become asexual do so because one or both have sustained hurt feelings due to neglect, poor communication, infidelity or workaholism. It should be

with Relationship Quality," *Archives of Sexual Behavior* 40, no. 2 (2011), 441–448.

said that 25% of all Americans (a third of women and a fifth of men) suffer from a condition known as hypoactive sexual desire (HSD), which is defined as a "persistent or recurring deficiency or absence of sexual fantasies or thoughts, or a lack of interest in sex or being sexual."[2]

However, as a holistic psychotherapist, I am cognizant of the fact that a persistent lack of sexual desire does not just appear in a vacuum. People who are consistently stressed out and overworked and do not prioritize their physical and emotional health often end up with a stunted libido. Also, we cannot ignore the fact that some medications, such as SSRIs (selective serotonin reuptake inhibitors), can affect sexual desire.

People with severe depression often need to deal with their depression by using SSRIs, which then takes precedence over dealing with the sexual-desire issue. This impacts a long-term relationship, though ideally only temporarily if they are able to over time, with support from their doctor, switch to natural supplements plus therapy to deal with their depression, and thus not incur the sexual side effects of the SSRIs.

Other reasons couples may become asexual include painful conditions such as vaginismus and erectile dysfunction as well as post-pregnancy issues and hormonal imbalances, which may or may not be temporary.

Some couples do manage to get through lack of sex caused by these conditions by deepening their emotional connection and finding other ways to ignite passion. Sex

---

[2] Stef Daniel, "Can a Relationship Survive on Little to No Sex?" *Professor's House*, 2015,
http://www.professorshouse.com/relationships/marriage-advice/articles/can-a-relationship-survive-on-little-to-no-sex.

therapy, energy work, vitamins and exercise are all part of the potential healing, but it takes discipline and hard work, and it doesn't always yield a happy ending.

As well, all long-term couples go through a dry spell from time to time; however, to become completely asexual is another story.

Studies suggest that this has a negative impact on the healthiness of a marriage in the long term.

According to Denise A. Donnelly, an associate professor of sociology at Georgia State University who has conducted studies on sexless marriages, "People in sexless marriages report that they are more likely to have considered divorce, and that they are less happy in their marriages."[3]

An American survey showed that "regular sexual activity in marriage is correlated to personal satisfaction, and men and women report higher levels of overall relationship happiness when they have more sex."[4]

A 2007 Pew Survey found that a "happy sexual relationship" was the second in importance, after "faithfulness," for marital satisfaction, with 70% of adults saying it was "very important" for a successful marriage.[5]

---

[3] Tara Parker-Pope, "When Sex Leaves the Marriage," *The New York Times*, June 3, 2009, http://well.blogs.nytimes.com/2009/06/03/when-sex-leaves-the-marriage/?_r=0.
[4] Thomas D. Williams, "Sexless Marriage in America Keeps Rising, New Study Reveals," *Breitbart*, January 2, 2015, http://www.breitbart.com/big-government/2015/01/02/sexless-marriage-in-america-keeps-rising-new-study-reveals.
[5] Pew Research Center, "Modern Marriage: 'I Like Hugs. I Like Kisses. But What I Really Love Is Help with the Dishes,'" July 18, 2007, http://www.pewsocialtrends.org/2007/07/18/modern-marriage.

Some Reasons Why People Cheat

Following are some of the reasons people give me for deciding to be unfaithful to their spouses:

- Not dealing with conflict in a healthy way with loss of respect and disdain for one another.
- The overfuctioner becoming resentful and tired of being in that role but cannot find a healthy way out.
- Not regarding one another positively.
- Completely ignoring each other.
- Taking each other for granted.
- Not noticing each other (not paying attention).
- Constantly operating from resentment.
- Not prioritizing each other.
- Taking each other for granted.
- Allowing touch and sex to drop off significantly.
- Not having sex at all.
- Not carving out time for each other.
- Having emotional affairs at work.
- Allowing oneself to feel valued and validated by other people.

Signs That It Might Be Time to Call It Quits

- Abuse. Addiction. Violence.
- A verbally violent and judgmental atmosphere.
- Relentless shaming and criticism.
- Yelling and screaming as the only way to communicate.
- Fear of discussing or inability to discuss problems.
- Partner won't solve problems or seek help for addictions
- Afraid to speak honestly. Never having an authentic voice in the relationship.
- Everyone constantly walking on eggshells. Fear of volatile emotional explosions.
- A partner who is constantly jealous for no reason.
- Violent and controlling behavior.

Chapter 11

Healthy Divorce: A Case Study

The case study that makes up this chapter is an example of a healthy divorce. It involves Celina (Cel) and Fred; their daughter, Samantha (Sam); and Sean, Celina's second partner. This family exemplifies how it is possible to go through a divorce in a mature, balanced and healthy way. I have known the family for many years, and I have always been impressed by the way they treat one another and how well adjusted Sam, now twelve years old, is.

We met one evening on Cel and Sean's backyard terrace for a lovely summer dinner. The whole family was there, and they were kind enough to allow me into their home and into their private lives to conduct an interview with them (transcribed below) on how they were able to maintain such peace and balance in their family through the years, even though there had been a divorce and a new relationship:

Victoria: How did you meet? How many years ago?

Fred: Almost thirty years ago. We were eighteen. We met through mutual friends, and we used to see each other at dance clubs. We had a one-night stand, never dated, then drifted apart for a while. Then Cel went to university and I went to Europe. We reconnected later through a mutual friend and started dating in '93 when I was twenty-four and Cel was twenty-three.

V: What drew you to each other at that point?

F: Good question.

Celina: I'd say we were opposites at the time. For me it was his calm and his humor, and he was the antithesis of my father. The energy he had was the exact opposite, and that appealed to me.

F: Probably the opposite for me. Cel had the spice that I was looking for. There was some energy that I was attracted to that I wasn't used to having around. There was a lot of humor — that was more of a similarity than a difference!

V: From that dating time, was it a tempestuous or a peaceful relationship? Did you fight a lot? What was the energy? Some serious questions here!

F: Let's go back. There was some combustion to the relationship I think. I was a bit more internal, and Cel was more external. Regarding coping skills to communicate in a healthier fashion, we kind of went off the rails at times with that. We hurt each other at times. I knew when she'd had enough and called me on it. She needed me to be more engaged in the relationship, in different ways. I probably had moments of frustration too; maybe I didn't voice them in that healthy a fashion. Part of the cycle we got into over time was that there would be conflict, some resolution, some peace and harmony — and there was no timeline to this — then a conflict again. For me, at least, we also had the best resolutions.

V: Cel, how did you two get to resolutions? What was the methodology?

C: How did we find our way? I think our lack of money at the time really bonded us. We would laugh at how poor we were — Kraft dinner! Those weren't the moments that caused us stress. It was the poor communication between us that caused us stress.

V: Did you lose respect for one another?

C: We weren't taught to communicate in a healthy way. We were young, we didn't know. I knew one way of communicating but he knew a different way — more non-communicative than communicative, that was the issue. So there was me, too much communication on one end, and him, not enough on the other. I was more

204

spontaneous, and he was much more serious. What attracted us to each other was that we were each other's opposites. For a time, we embraced those qualities in each other. I remember one time we wanted to go skiing, and I said, "Just call in sick. We'll go skiing for one day." It was really hard for him to make that phone call. We had a huge fight about it. It was a big deal for him taking any time off work. For me it wasn't. I guess real opposites in that regard.

V: How did you resolve these differences?

C: That came later. I know he liked my sense of adventure, so he would jump on board for my fun ideas. But it was always me pushing in that direction. He would call in sick, have that day and live that day. We were both professionals, heading in that upwardly mobile direction of the common couple. Then a shift in me happened with my job in advertising, where I was questioning everything about my life, I quit my job and started therapy because I just wasn't happy. I started questioning and learning and all that. And then, eventually, once I went into my own individual therapy, I had to realize that he couldn't do everything I asked of him. I needed to stop pushing him.

V: What I'm hearing is that until you went into personal therapy, he would give in to you. What else happened when you started to do your personal work?

C: There wasn't a lot of fighting at that time. There was a lot of pain and misunderstanding of what was really happening in our relationship. As I started to really shift, I would say to myself, "Fred is going to join that awakening of therapy and awareness — or not." Thankfully, he chose to go to individual therapy as well.

V: You, Fred, went to your own therapy to process? Was that helpful?

F: Yes, yes it was. In all honesty, initially I did it for the relationship – to save the relationship. I walked in thinking that, but in time I found that there was work I wanted to do for me. But that wasn't my initial motivation. The therapy unearthed a lot of things for me. Cel and I were each uncovering things personally. She had her own issues that were simmering and not being dealt with, and so did I. It started to come to the surface for both of us.

C: We separated for a while.

V: Trial separation?

F: We had a trial separation, where we didn't live apart, but I moved into the other room. There were intimacy factors going on; there was a disconnect, and we discovered we needed a time out from each other in a big way.

V: What did you get out of the trial separation? How long did it last?

C: Way less than a year — six months or so.

V: Did that lead to the eventual demise of the relationship, or do you think it was therapeutic? Because sometimes I do recommend therapeutic separations to get a little perspective.

C: During that time, I remember we were knee-deep in understanding codependency. The individual therapy was so instrumental for both of us and actually was the trigger that we both needed to really latch onto in order to understand the profound codependency we were both living in our relationship.

V: What did you understand about codependency with regard to your relationship?

C: We both realized that we were relying on the other person for emotional boosting. Having to rely on the other person to make you feel better, whether by act, words, intention or whatever is not healthy. It becomes a burden.

F: For me, codependency was something I was probably seeking at that stage in my life. Here was this person who seemed controlling but who seemingly had her stuff together, and I sought out what appeared to be strength. She had strength of character. We got into a pattern where Cel made all the social decisions. I was dependent on that. If we went on a trip, or bought a car, Cel initiated it. It became a pattern, and I wasn't happy at a deep level with it. It wasn't anyone's fault — not her fault that I didn't speak up and use my voice; it was just the pattern playing on itself over and over. Once I was in therapy, I was then able to better understand the codependency in our relationship and, quite frankly, my lack of self-love. I didn't know how to love myself very well. I still struggle with that.

V: Was that a family-culture issue?

F: Yes, my family upbringing — shame and the lovely baggage that people have. I hadn't healed a lot of it or been aware of it until I went through therapy and really started to evaluate our exchanges as a couple. Cel was also experiencing this and being challenged by it in her own family. She called her family on the carpet with stuff. Her strength of character, which is part of Cel's DNA, was going out to get answers from family members who had conditioned her in a certain way, and I don't think they were ready to face some of the questions she had. I sat there and said, "Wow, that's an approach!" But it was very different from my approach.

C: At that point I remember I needed to create some real distance, so I decided to travel to Los Angeles for a while. When I came back, we reconnected for a couple of months, with intimacy again, and we soon realized I was pregnant! It was a real surprise for us because I didn't think I could get pregnant. We'd been together for so long having unprotected sex, and I had never managed to become pregnant. So this was a big surprise!

F: A complete surprise. I had forgotten that it had happened not too long after the trial separation.

C: Something is surfacing for me right now as we are talking. I recognize in both of us that there was a "high" that happens with therapy, when you start discovering yourself and really understanding "this is why I do this." Both of us, when we were reconnecting, went into that high, which assisted in our reconnecting post-separation.

V: That makes sense, Cel. You were both doing therapy and discovering what makes you both tick as well as understanding where all the patterns were coming from. You were sharing it with each other, and, of course, that would bring you to feeling more connected at that time. Did that solidify the relationship for the next while?

F: It may have. That's a good question. I think it reconnected us in a good "oh wow!" kind of way. A big step in growing up for us, and for a lot of people. When you're presented with having a child, it's a big wake-up call and an even bigger wake-up call when you did not think that medically this could happen for you.

C: I was told I couldn't have kids.

V: I can see how that would be incredibly shocking to both of you and a real turning point as well.

C: And at that point, we started to really look into the commitment to each other as we were very excited to "be the change." We knew we were going to heal by "being the change."

V: And it sounds as though you were able to hold onto that for a while.

C: I think ever since.

F: In some respects we have. The relationship still had cracks. But since then we have always been committed to the process of "being the change"; that is, not falling back on old patterns, whether we were together or not.

V: But what I'm hearing you say is that there was a foundation from the personal work you did that still remains today, even though you are not together, a foundation of non-codependency and commitment to self-responsibility, regardless.

C: I don't want this to sound like a fairytale. There was never just one side to this. There were moments, with the initial rejection by him, where I felt rejection since he was the one who said "we're done."

V: You initiated the final break of the relationship, Fred?

F: Correct. I was the one who created the catharsis to the final break up. I will never forget that moment that February when I told Cel that I felt I needed to separate from our relationship.

V: What was in you that said "it's gotta stop"? Was there that moment?

F: That took some time! She asked the same question: "Why? What's behind all this feeling?" For as much work as I thought I had done on my self-esteem, I had always felt I could never live up to her standards. She pleaded with me on that and said it wasn't true, but for me that was something that was just there.

V: This was an underlying feeling within yourself?

F: I realized ultimately that this was a key dynamic in our relationship. I'm not saying that she's to blame. We had and have a lot of respect for one another, but I could not deny how different we were from each other. Our differences as people maybe started coming out through therapy and solidified as time went on, especially by having a child.

C: And it was also the parenting styles.

V: What do you mean by that?

C: I think we were opposites when it came to parenting as well. It's okay to be opposites when it's just two people who can create that fun for one another, but when Samantha came, that knocked us out. As much as we were excited about it, when the reality hit, it was heartbreaking to know that we didn't have a support system at all. It was just the two of us. And I didn't handle that well at all. His mother was bipolar, and unavailable. My mother was emotionally absent. It was just very stressful. I went into knee-deep nurture mode, and he went into knee-deep protector/provider mode. I remember fighting with him because he would come home late, and I was exhausted. I would demand, "Why the hell are you late?" And he would say, "Well, I want to be the number-one salesman this year." I could not believe that he picked this year to be the number-one salesperson, but what I wasn't seeing was that he was functioning on a total "Male. Provider. I gotta work" level. At the time, because looking after the baby was stressful, I didn't realize he wasn't doing this to hurt me or to not be with the baby. Today I realize that he needed to find ways to support these two women he loved deeply. I didn't manage that well at all. It was very difficult.

V: Did it get ugly?

F: I'll be honest. Cel's way more comfortable with confrontation than I am, and some of that cycle of bad communicating reared its ugly head. But when we recognized this, we wanted to stop the cycle of dysfunction; we always made our daughter and the environment she was going to grow up in priority one.

V: What decisions did you both make that indicated Samantha is priority one — regarding how you negotiated conflict or decisions you made?

C: To me, it was communicating with him with the idea that he is the father of my child, not my ex-husband, whom I had issues with. And he was incredibly generous with his time after work, especially when I was exhausted from being the only parent all day and all night. Before work, he'd come over early to spend time with her, then go to work, and come after work to spend time with her.

V: It sounds as if you have a lot of respect for Sam's dad.

C: Absolutely. It's that distinction between *this* relationship and the family relationship that didn't work. Family relationship is what needs to be constantly fed, and we both understood this distinction clearly.

V: Were there any moments of contention or issues between the two of you that would bleed into the family relationship?

C: Of course! We are not perfect! But we found a way to always maintain our respect for one another.

V: You never seemed to allow the conflicts to go deeply into disrespectful communication all in the name of keeping the family happy and healthy.

C: Even when we had problems communicating, we made our home the nest where Sam would remain, and we would come back and forth, always making sure that Sam was at peace because we didn't want her to feel the energetic quality of the separation.

V: You were mindful of that.

C: Yes. We never did anything that was damaging to each other, nothing long term. It was a big deal because Fred was a product of divorce and knew what that feeling and texture felt like.

V: So Sam was two when you split? How old is she now?

C: Twelve.

V: I understand you still do family dinnertimes.

C: Yes. Mondays and Wednesdays are family dinnertime. We wanted to soften the separation a bit for her. We realized within a year that she was always in a state of missing one of us. So we decided to give her moments, dinners at least, when she wasn't missing one of us. I think that was tremendous in filling in her heart after seeing her parents breaking up.

V: I love that you both did that. I wanted to ask, how did you maintain such relative peace even on the financial questions? How did you come to those agreements?

F: Initially, the financial reality didn't really change. What was being paid for rent and for Sam's upkeep didn't change. That was one of the reasons I moved in with my family initially, because I couldn't afford another place. We didn't have assets to split up, no house to sell.

V: That simplified things. Had there been assets, do you think it would have been more contentious?

C: No, because even had there been assets, we would've been equally respectful about them. Again, we wanted to maintain the same level of respect, even in this area, especially because we'd agreed when I was pregnant that I would be staying home instead of using daycare.

V: You both agreed to that?

F and C: Yes.

F: It was always a strain on me financially, but, as much as I could, I didn't want to make anything uncomfortable for either of them. I was the one who left the relationship, so there was some guilt tied to all of this, but only initially. I also grew up in an environment where my mother divorced my father, and he didn't pay a dime. And she never chose to go after him. The world was different back then in the 'Seventies. At that time, for the primary wage earner, usually the father, child-support issues were different.

V: It sounds as though you suffered from that.

F: Well, yeah. I saw my mom's level of resentment and how it affected me. And she realized she did it to herself because she never fought for it, and she could have.

V: So you chose, based on your influences from home, to go a different way. It sounds as though you were consciously deciding in an integrity-oriented way not to adversely affect your child or the mother of your child.

F: Yes. And it was hard.

V: Yes, but most good choices are hard to make. You both could have descended into the pit of mudslinging, but you chose not to. You guys seem balanced about it, but, of course, you're human, and sometimes there are contentious issues.

F: It's one area we've been able to keep consistent. We never really rocked the boat. Neither of us wanted to.

V: Because it was working.

C: Another note on money that's important is that there were moments that were tough, such as during his career changes, I do believe that Fred always felt comfortable to come to me and say, "Listen, I haven't got a job yet. We might have to discuss money," and I was always okay with this. He didn't have to deal with the fear that if anything went wrong, I would be unfair to him.

V: Cel, I imagine things also changed when you brought to your life a new partner, Sean.

C: Yes. And once Sean came into the picture, the finances also changed a little bit, and there was more of a shared experience financially once he started to live here.

V: When did the dynamic change? When did you and Sean start to see each other?

C: About nine-and-a-half years ago.

V: Basically, Sean, you have been in this family since Sam was three. You are an integral part of this family.

Sean: At this point, I definitely feel as though I am.

V: You two aren't married, but you live together in a stable relationship. You're basically Sam's step-dad.

S: Yes.

V: She has two dads. That's phenomenal. Sometimes that doesn't work, but it seems to work in this family.

S: It was a slow progression of spending time with her, developing that relationship.

V: Was it ever contentious between you and Sam?

S: Never. In the first ten minutes, she grabbed my hand.

C: It was unbelievable.

V: That's pretty special.

C: The slow integration that influenced all of us was the affection that Sean and I showed toward one another. I think this was really big because Sam never saw affection between Fred and me when she was small.

When Sam witnessed Sean and me hugging, she became more affectionate with Fred as a result. That was pretty special. But all this took its time. She didn't meet him until about nine months into our relationship, not even fully until after a year. It was a slow process. Not just for Sam's well-being, but for all of ours as well.

V: You were not impulsive.

S: I am an impulsive person by nature, but in this case, maturity and experience helped me slow down and evaluate what I really wanted for myself and what was best for the child.

C: There were times when Sean held back from deepening his relationship with Sam because he didn't want to cause any harm between Fred and Sam.

S: I didn't *need* to be her father.

V: Yet you've become one of her fathers.

S: Yes. And I never did anything consciously to try to make her love me.

V: Sean, you and Fred get along?

S: Absolutely.

V: How do you feel about fitting into this dynamic of this family? How does it feel for you?

S: At first it felt as though I was coming into something in which I did not know what my place was. I wasn't trying to carve out anything. I just wanted to be a positive energy within it.

V: How did you conclude that you wanted to be a positive influence on this situation?

S: I think it comes through the extreme pain of my own first family's breaking up. I also have many nieces, nephews and great-nephews and nieces, so I've had a lot of family around me, and I value that. And I value seeing the world through the eyes of a child.

V: It sounds as though you'd come from a painful breakup.

S: Yes. I was married for five years and had a very bitter, hard-fought divorce.

V: You knew you didn't want to contribute to that happening in this family.

S: And I was parentally alienated from my own child through that divorce.

V: So painful. Just tragic.

S: I feel that it is tragic for my child as well.

V: Sean, I'm so impressed that you were able to come through the pain and to have it influence you in a way that you can actually learn from it. The big difference I see here with this family is that everyone is attempting to learn from their pasts. You aren't just blindly repeating the past. You are all willing to learn from it, and that is a big message here.

C: Eventually, we made sure we included Sean in our great family dinners. One of the things with Sean is that before the dinners, he saw the respect Fred and I had for each other. He fell more in love with me almost because of how I treated Fred, and vice versa. The respect was established from the get-go.

V: There was a strong foundation of respect.

C: Yes, and we all used our history to feed that respect. Fred and I appreciated our lives even more because we knew from Sean how it can turn ugly, and you can lose it just like that. We never took it for granted.

V: Nine years later, from my vantage point, you are a family of three parents with one child, not two parents and the boyfriend — three integral parts of this family, equally influencing the development of a healthy family dynamic that is positive for everyone, including this child. Sean, did you do any personal therapy work?

S: Yes. I had to work on my own pain from my previous marriage, but that helped me in this relationship. I did some self-evaluation, looking in the mirror.

V: Taking personal responsibility is a major theme here. It's not about having no bumps in the road. But through those bumps, you're looking at yourself and taking responsibility for your own words, actions, feelings, not blaming or projecting too much.

S: It's very difficult to have all those filters in place all the time, but they're there, and they're of value.

V: What about careful, or, better said, mindful, communication? You're all very human, and I love that! But long-term passionate and successful relationships happen by being careful and mindful in communication, not taking each other for granted, hurling remarks that are passive-aggressive or unkind — it happens, but then you take personal responsibility and apologize when needed.

At this point, Cel, Fred, and Sean left the terrace, and Samantha came out to sit with me.

V: Hello, Sam, thank you for coming out and joining me for a little one-on-one talk. How old are you?

Sam: Twelve.

V: What's life like for you with regard to your parents and their separation? Sean has been in your life since you were three, right? It's like you have two dads? How has this whole experience been for you?

Sam: Because of the way my parents handled it, it's been great. I'm happy they divorced because otherwise they'd be fighting every day.

V: How do you feel about Sean?

Sam: He's great. He really lets me talk about anything and not feel uncomfortable.

V: It sounds as though you don't hold any resentment toward your mother or father.

Sam: No. They've made it healthy for me, and they've made me understand why they divorced, and I've adapted to that, and I've understood that.

V: Is there anything you'd like to share with me about your parents' divorce and how they managed it with your family dinners, including having Sean at some of those dinners?

Sam: I think the family dinners are great because it lets me understand that although they're divorced and live in separate houses, I can still have that family connection, and they can be together. I'm happy they created that healthy lifestyle. We are a family.

V: You always have a sense of family, not separateness, with both of them.

Sam: Yeah. I think it's also good for Sean because of his past. I think it is good for him to have that family feeling. He understands that I spend time with my dad and my mom and that he is also a part of that, which I'm happy about.

V: Okay, guys, you can all come back. One last question for you, Fred. Do you ever feel any contention or discomfort around Sean?

F: No. He's a good person. He's really good to my daughter, which is important to me, and he's good to my ex, and he's always been positive, even in moments of any tension, which he'd respectfully stay out of as well.

V: You see it as a priority to be good to your ex. Why?

F: Sure! Because we may not have worked out, but she's a human being, she's got a big heart, she's the mother of my child. I want her to be emotionally healthy, doing good things for her life, because it'll help not only her but also our daughter to be around that. I have no ill will. I want contentment for her.

V: Do you have any final comments, Celina, on this healthy divorce?

C: Make the right choice, not the easy one! Because it produces a positive result, every time.

V: Beautiful. Sean, any last thoughts?

S: Stay strong; don't give into the impulse.

V: Because?

S: It can have a very negative effect.

V: Impulsiveness is your enemy.

S: Well put.

V: This is amazing. You as a family are an example that I refer to in my practice when I work with people who are going through difficult times in their relationships and are heading toward divorce. I talk about this family, and I hope your ears aren't burning! Thanks again for sharing your story with us and for all of this precious information.

Celina, Fred and Sean all did the difficult thing of not repeating their family-cultures.

They chose not to perpetuate the cycle of dysfunction, thus saving Samantha from repeating unhealthy patterns in her relationships.

Furthermore, they chose to establish a new normal — a new relationship-culture.

Even though this was a divorce, they were all still in a relationship, and so they were establishing a new relationship-culture, whether they intended to or not.

They could have allowed a dysfunctional relationship-culture to ensue. But no, this family decided that the pain of the past needed to be neutralized and replaced with a kind of connection that was nurturing and healthy. And this is not an easy thing to do.

Many people succumb to the undisciplined, impulsive choice of simply letting the resentments, hurt feelings and perceived injustices take over.

This then feeds each person's hurt child, which, in turn, makes that child react in a tantrum-like way that ultimately leads to decisions that hurt the family, and that are then repeated generation after generation.

Just because you are divorcing does not mean you have the right to hurl your patterns of dysfunction onto the next generation.

This family decided they would continue doing the difficult thing of promoting respect, friendship, consideration, mindfulness and consciousness as a way to live.

It was my privilege to be invited into this home to witness a family that was determined to remain so conscious and aware of every action. I know that this is possible to do.

I am not saying that they never had challenges. It was evident that they did. Everyone does.

However, they decided that the buck stopped with them. The cycle of dysfunction stopped with them.

This family makes that decision every single day, over and over.

This is what is required; the decisions need to be made consciously every day so as not to repeat the old patterns of toxicity and dysfunction.

That is how you rewire your relationship-culture.

Every day in every way you make conscious and aware decisions to improve your quality of life and leave a positive legacy for the next generation.

Conclusion
The Alchemy of Life

A quote from one of my favorite books, *The Alchemist*, by Paulo Coelho goes like this: "'This is why alchemy exists,' the boy said. 'So that everyone will search for his treasure, find it, and then want to be better than he was in his former life. ... When we strive to become better than we are, everything around us becomes better, too.'"[1]

I absolutely love this quote! *The Alchemist* speaks to the very concept I talk about at length in this book: We are like alchemists searching for our treasures — our profound and healthy relationships. And it is through this search that we can become inspired to transform ourselves and our relationships into better versions so that we can impact the people in our lives and our surroundings in positive ways.

We can take responsibility for ourselves, and we can decide to grow beyond what we have learned. We can rewire every belief that we inherited from our family-culture through intention, awareness and repetition. We can engage the new awareness through performing deliberate actions and making deliberate decisions over and over until our neural pathways reflect those changes and our lives embody those shifts. This then creates a new normal, a new pattern, a new way of being.

When you choose to rewire your relationship-culture, you are, in effect, deciding that the connection you have with the people in your life is going to be different from what

---

[1] Paul Coelho, *The Alchemist: A Fable about Following Your Dream* (San Francisco: HarperCollins, 1993), 158.

you learned multigenerationally. And, of course, you're changing only what is not healthy, functional or helpful. You *can* do this. You *can* rewire your relationship-culture. You *can* create a new normal. The question is, will you do the work that is required? Will you go on the journey to search for your treasure — a happy, healthy, passionate, connected relationship-culture? Will you decide that you no longer want to repeat the relationship patterns that you learned from your family-culture that were not healthy or functional? Will you repeat this new awareness over and over until it becomes the new normal? If your answer is yes to these questions, then you are deciding that the buck stops with you! That the cycle of dysfunction stops with *you*. And that *you* are going to successfully halt generations of dysfunctional relationships and families by rewiring your relationship-culture!

Rewiring your relationship-culture so that it is a healthy one has far-reaching positive effects and requires that you walk a fine line, balancing between self-care and relationship-care. Whether you are dating or in a committed relationship, you cannot focus only on yourself; conversely, you also cannot focus exclusively on your relationship. The attention that you dole out needs to be equally given to both aspects. You also need to go about the business of knowing yourself deeply so that you are not living from a false self. You need to know *what* your patterns are and *how* they are affecting you so that you can clean up whatever is needed. This ensures that you attract the right partner toward yourself and that you make good decisions within your relationships.

The process of changing your patterns and behaviors involves understanding that your brain is an elegant machine. Science has determined that your brain's plasticity serves you wonderfully since it is changeable and responsive to new experiences and habits. The brain is able to reorganize itself by forming new connections (neural pathways) every time you develop a new way of doing something and a new pattern of behavior, especially if you practice the new behavior often. It is nature's way of supporting us when we try to make good changes for ourselves. However, remember that the brain is also just as (and possibly even more) receptive to negative patterns and repetitions. So it is your job to decide what you need to change and how you want your brain to rewire itself so that it is conducive to positive ways of being.

And, of course, we cannot have a good relationship with others if the relationship with ourselves has gone off the rails. Getting in right relationship with yourself means working diligently to clean up any dynamics that are vestiges of the hurt child trying to survive. It means learning about good boundary communication and committing to neutralizing patterns of guilt, manipulation, shame, judgment, control, codependency, jealousy, lying, cheating and so much more.

It means taming your inner bully, valuing yourself, being emotionally self-sufficient and awakening your inner positive cheerleading coach. It means stopping any patterns of emotional dumpster diving, overfunctioning, infantilizing and parentifying, and also not succumbing to addictions of any kind, including codependency, which forces a person to live and die by the "disease-to-please" lifestyle. It also means not falling in love with someone's potential and being keenly attentive to and staying away from such destructive patterns as jealousy, commitment phobia and narcissism. Part of that process means that you need to step fully into your adult self and take personal responsibility for everything that is going on in your life now. When you enter the dating and relationship realms, I invite you to take personal responsibility for how you navigate your relationships and how you communicate with others. Yes, it is true that we all make mistakes. However, the adult takes responsibility for those mistake and goes about the business of repairing the damage done. Being in your adult self trumps all manner of impulsiveness that is born from the unresolved hurt child within.

And then when you finally do meet the right person, being in your full adult self means bravely navigating through a process so that you understand each other's truths. Before marriage, you decide to find out where each other stands regarding sex, money, family relationships, children, lifestyle and communication. All this so you don't blindly enter marriage without having a clear understanding about these key areas, which, if left hidden under the carpet of denial, could later come to haunt a relationship and drive it down Divorce Drive.

Also, once you do get into that great relationship that you worked diligently to be ready for and decide to marry, it behooves you to learn the skills and tools to fight fairly so that you contribute to the cleanup of the relationship versus the mess! The "Initiate and Reflect" exercise that I discuss in Chapter 8 is one of the best methodologies I know of that is fundamental to the successful navigation through your triggers, hurt feelings, conflicts and anger.

Also, so that your relationship stays compelling and fun, I invite you to make sure that you and your partner honor each other, become each other's best friends and cheerleaders, express yourselves daily through humor, sensual touch and random acts of kindness. I ask that you prioritize frequent sexuality so that the associated neural pathways stay alive and healthy for the long haul so that your intimacy deepens more and more over time. I task you with impacting your partner and your relationship in positive ways five times more often than in negative ways. Since the brain is infinitely more porous to negative events, this ratio is crucial to maintain throughout a marriage. As a result, you happily build up a pot of goodwill that brims over with a surplus of positivity that carries you through the bumpy and painful times of life.

It's true that the kinds of relationships I think are worth fighting for are not drama-filled like the Hollywood-endorsed relationships people frequently see today. I am speaking of the stuff of creating long-term, healthy, functional, passionate relationships that can stand the test of time and provide a healing elixir that can quite possibly render neutral and harmless a multigenerational destructive and dysfunctional pattern.

With all this, you get to celebrate the fact that it was *you* who decided to make a difference. It was *you* who decided to make sure that you, your partner, the relationship you chose to create and the children you decided to have would be healthy. It was *you* who pursued the process of rewiring your relationship-culture.

And due to the self-love you chose to foster in yourself, *you* decided that you were not going to hurl onto the future generations everything that was hurled onto you. You decided that you would live a life of good relationships that was accountable, healthy, vulnerable, authentic, respectful, passionate and loving.

Well, I say bravo! I tip my hat off to you if you are one of those people who refuses to succumb to living a life that is less than what is your due, but who chooses to live a life that is filled with the richness of a healthy, sane, happy, passionate relationship-culture.

About the Author
Victoria Lorient-Faibish,
RP, MEd (Psych), CCC, RPP, BCPP, RPE

As a registered psychotherapist, keynote speaker, author, holistic psychotherapist, relationship expert and life and wellness coach with a busy practice in Toronto, Victoria has been inspiring people to find their self-cultures, rewire their relationship-cultures, step into their personal power, speak more authentically and fully embrace their life purposes since 1990.

Victoria feels honored and humbled to do the work she does. She has studied and practiced Eastern philosophy modalities for over eight years, and she has a master's degree in educational psychology to round out her experience and knowledge.

As well, Victoria is a registered member of the College of Psychotherapists of Ontario, a certified member of the Canadian Counseling and Psychotherapy Association and a board-certified polarity therapy practitioner and teacher as well as a reiki master and a practitioner of New Decision Therapy.

Connecting – Rewire Your Relationship Culture (Manor House) is the author's second book, following her first release: *Find Your 'Self Culture' – Moving from Depression and Anxiety to Monumental Self-Acceptance.*

Victoria resides with her husband Kevin in Toronto, where she also runs a busy and successful psychotherapy practice.

Appendices

Appendix A
Visualization to Increase Self-Esteem

Use this visualization exercise to help increase your self-esteem. To fully relax into it, I recommend that you record the text, reading slowly, so you can have your eyes closed while you play it back.

Sit or lie comfortably and close your eyes. Inhale slowly through your nose to fill your lungs, and then exhale through your nose. Continue this slow, circular breathing while you imagine that you are on the top of a mountain, a fantastically beautiful mountain overlooking the world.

You can feel the breeze on your skin and hair. You can smell the crisp, clean air. In the distance you see a group of fluffy clouds, and they're slowly coming toward you. They're getting closer and closer and closer. Now they are at your eye level. Sitting on top of a cloud is your power animal. Your significant power animal, which will communicate with you, is sitting there. Look at it. What is your animal? Let that animal gaze at you as you gaze at it.

Let that animal be there peacefully, shining its love and affection and wisdom on you. All of a sudden, that animal sends you a thought bubble, which clearly says, "You are loved. You are valuable. You have a right to have needs, to have feelings. You are worthwhile." Just take that energy in from that power animal. Let that entire message wash through every cell and molecule of your body. Allow each cell, each atom, each molecule to receive the message that you are loved, you are valuable, you have a right to your feelings and thoughts, and you're open to receiving love in a healthy way. You're open to receiving affection and kindness. Feel that thought wash through you. Take the time to allow that message to sink into to your very core.

Take a number of deep breathes, in and out, and linger with the feeling that you are a precious, valuable and lovable being and that you deserve to have healthy, positive, loving and functional relationships in your life.

As you look at the cloud and your animal, they gradually begin to move away until they are out of sight, but that concept has imprinted itself in you and in all of your cells and atoms. Take a moment to say farewell to this beautiful cloud and your animal that gave you that information, knowing that you simply need to call upon it for it to reappear.

You are back, standing on the top of the mountain. You spread your arms, and you feel a sense of connection to the planet, to the Universe and to the divine, all the while feeling extremely grounded and connected to planet Earth. It is a dual feeling of connection to planet Earth and groundedness and, at the same time, a deep connection to the divine and the Universe — the two polarities sending you their energy.

Slowly open your eyes and gently stretch. As you bring your awareness back to your surroundings, you continue to feel grounded yet connected to the divine. You allow the sensation of self-love and self-acceptance to stay with you deeply at your core. Give yourself a hug and say to yourself, "I love you and I honor you."

Appendix B

Visualization to Transform Your Inner Bully
Into a Supportive Coach

I recommend you record this visualization text, reading it slowly, so you can relax with your eyes closed while you play it back. Have a pen and paper handy to write on. Sit in a calm space and close your eyes. Imagine yourself in a peaceful, natural setting. Call forth the bully in you; for example, imagine a schoolyard bully. In your mind's eye, invite the bully to sit down with you. Be open and non-judgmental as you ask the bully the following key questions and wait patiently for the responses:

1.   What are you *trying* to do for me? How are you trying to help me by continually showing up in my life? (Pause. Breathe. Write.)

2.   What is your positive purpose in my life? (Pause. Breathe. Write.)

3.   What do you seek to accomplish for me by constantly being in my life? (Pause. Breathe. Write.)

Once you've heard the answers to your questions, you can tell the bully you understand what it is trying to do for you. You can say, "Bully, I know you might be trying to protect me from failure and disappointment, and you're trying to encourage me to be the best I can be; however, as you know, you are failing miserably at this task due to your abusive tone. Your way is not effective." (Pause) "I want to thank you for your efforts, but a new way is needed now." Continue to visualize the bully slowly becoming a more positive version of itself — a supportive and encouraging coach. Imagine this inner coach in detail, allowing its gentle, encouraging — yet strong — voice to emerge. Your coach now says to you, "I believe in you," "You are precious and lovable, and you deserve gentleness as you ease into your transitions," "Bit by bit you're getting to your goal" and "Consistency is the key to your success. Stick with it. I know you can do it. I believe in you!"

Appendix C

Visualization to Heal the Cycle of Self-Denial

I recommend that you record this visualization, reading it slowly, so you can have your eyes closed and fully relax while you play it back.

Sit comfortably and close your eyes. Slow your breathing down. Take a few minutes to focus on your breath. Imagine yourself standing somewhere beautiful in nature, perhaps on your own beach, in a forest or at the base of a mountain. Allow yourself the luxury of being fully in that space. Use your senses to take in the color of the sky, the color of the ground. Feel the wind on your face and feel yourself begin to walk comfortably.

In the distance, you see a house. Walk toward it. You are intrigued by how familiar the house looks. It is exactly how you would like it to be. It is your sanctuary — a beautiful, peaceful place that you can come back to again and again.

You come right up to the door, and you open it and walk in, and you see a comfortable place to sit in the living room. The room is warm, inviting and aesthetically pleasing. Take a moment to sit down and take everything in. Soon you begin to feel enveloped by a maternal energy. You can choose a maternal image or being from literature; or an archangel; or Mother Mary; or Quan Yin, the goddess of compassion or any other maternal image or being that you choose.

Bring that compassionate-mother energy into this room. Feel her behind you as if you were lying on her chest and her arms were around you. You feel a profound sense of safety and nurturing. Feel this maternal energy nourishing you, giving you everything you need, filling your soul — perhaps for the first time — with a sense of complete maternal safety. Imagine that all of your cells are absorbing that messaging of maternal safety.

Bring yourself as a four- or five-year-old child into the room. See the maternal mother invite the child to come and sit on your lap and lean on you. You are leaning onto the maternal energy as well, so there are three of you.

Feel that you are transmitting to the child that incredible nurturing and safety and healing, fully giving that female mother energy to that child through you — that complete sense of "You have the right to live. You have the right to be alive. You have a right to be here. You are loved unconditionally."

Feel all the cells of that child take in that energy, fully nurturing that child because you yourself feel fully nurtured by that maternal energy as well. Now say the words "I have a right to have needs. My needs and wants matter. I make myself a priority." Truly feel it and know at a deep, cellular level that you have a right to have needs and to draw boundaries. Know you matter and that you are precious and valuable.

Take a snapshot of the scene and memorize the details of the mother energy nurturing you, and you nurturing the child. Put that snapshot inside your heart so you can carry it with you.

And now, slowly open your eyes, but feel how this visualization has caused something to shift inside you.

Appendix D

Visualization to Reparent Yourself
and Heal the Hurt Child

The only real way to move beyond the scars of your upbringing and the anger you may have for your parents is to reparent yourself.

You need to make yourself a priority and treat yourself as you wish you had been treated as a child. You need to learn to be kind, loving, compassionate and forgiving toward yourself.

With daily repetition and the resulting laying down of new neural pathways, this exercise will allow you to heal the wounds of the past. Only then will you be able to move into a real adulthood, in which you need very little from your parents.

I recommend that you do this visualization every night before you fall asleep and repeat the affirmations at the end of the exercise often. If you do this, you will begin to make choices that demonstrate that you consider yourself to be a valuable person.

You will be discerning about the choices you make.

You will show the child within that you can be trusted to be a loving and responsible parent to yourself.

In time, you will have retrained your whole being to be self-loving and self-nurturing.

Before beginning this visualization, I recommend that you record it first, reading it slowly, so you can have your eyes closed and fully relax while you play it back.

Sit or lie comfortably and quietly in a room by yourself. Slow your breathing down and allow yourself to focus in on your breath for a few minutes. Imagine yourself as a child. Pick an age (preferably under the age of eight) that is significant to you, such as the first time you felt alone, or the first time you realized that not everything in life would go smoothly.

Imagine yourself taking care of yourself as a little child. See yourself giving this child within your unconditional, nurturing love. See yourself being the parent you needed and didn't have.

Imagine yourself as the calm and patient parent taking part in activities with the child; for example, gently brushing the child's hair, building a sand castle together, pushing the happy child on a swing or riding a merry-go-round together and laughing.

Say to yourself as a child, "You are enough. You matter. You are important to me. You are talented and beautiful, and I love you. I will always love you. You can count on me now." And then affirm to yourself, "I am enough." "I have enough." "There is more than enough in the Universe for me."

Allow these affirmations to go to your core; they work to fill feelings of emptiness and loneliness.

Appendix E
Exercise for Developing Your Self-Culture

Your *self-culture* is your authentic, instinctive self. The planet needs the real you; it's time you began the journey! The pursuit of self-culture is a hard one for many of us, and I have unlimited compassion for those who embark on this path. The quest for your self-culture is not a narcissistic, futile, self-indulgent pursuit. It is vital to your well-being. You can serve those you love and the planet better when you know who you are and are at peace with yourself. This peace does not come without the "spiritual warrior" part of you doing its finest battle on your behalf. The journey is a profound, and at times arduous, look within. The result will be an emerging self that you will treasure, savor and protect because you know you fought for it and won!

I recommend that you record the instructions, reading them slowly, so you can have your eyes closed and fully relax while you play it back. Have a pen and paper handy so you can write as well. Sit quietly in a comfortable chair at a writing surface. Close your eyes and breathe slowly and continuously without pauses so as soon as you get to the top of the inhale, begin to exhale, and when you get to the bottom of the exhale, begin to inhale. Repeat this pattern five times, and then open your eyes and ask yourself the following questions, taking your time to answer each one. Allow your inner voice to come up, and be honest and non-judgmental with yourself as you write down your answers:
1.   What "part" of myself am I not living? (Pause. Breathe. Write.)
2.   What do I long to express, explore and bring to light at this moment in my life? (Pause. Breathe. Write.)
3.   What makes my heart happy? What brings me joy? (Pause. Breathe. Write.)

4. Who is the real me? (Pause. Breathe. Write.)
5. What path do I long to be on? (Pause. Breathe. Write.)
6. How do I want to live my life? (Pause. Breathe, Write.)
7. What in my self-culture, my authentic self, do I need to unearth? (Pause. Breathe. Write.)
8. Who am I really? (Pause. Breathe. Write.)

You need to know the answers to these questions to live your life in the best way you can. As you answer them, you will begin to see the real you coming to life on the page. Now you can work with what you have written to explore even further. Read over your answers and try to come up with two or three sentences that describe what you have expressed. These will become your self-culture mission statements. Begin each sentence with "I" and write them clearly and concisely in the present tense. For example, you might write the following:

1. I now draw clear boundaries in my life, especially with my partner.
2. I am committed to treating myself as a priority and with kindness.
3. I now allow myself to explore all of my creativity in all that do.
4. I allow only balanced, healthy people in my inner circle.
5. I am now strong and centered.
6. I am able to take good care of myself at all times.
7. I feel empowered to say no whenever I need to.
8. I fill my own cup first, and I give to others only from the overflow.

Once you've written your self-culture mission statements, I encourage you to say them daily as part of a routine. Put copies of the statements in your bathroom and computer area, and keep a copy in your purse or wallet. Say it often. It is also helpful to visualize yourself living a life that embodies the core of these self-culture mission statements.

Appendix F

Exercise for Anchoring New Neural Pathways

Neural Pathways: The Biology of Change

As you begin your journey of transformation, it is helpful to understand the part your brain plays when you try to change beliefs and old patterns of behavior. The brain has thin neural pathways and thick ones; they could be compared to footpaths and highways.

Your long-held beliefs and behavior patterns, those that are inherited and learned through your society, family-culture and family dynamics, are ingrained in the wide, complex highway networks of your neural pathways, whereas newer beliefs and behavior patterns form in simple, narrow footpaths in your brain. The former are harder to change because, having been there so long, buried in your unconscious, you act without self-awareness according to your long-held beliefs and behavior patterns.

In his book *The Brain That Changes Itself: Stories of Personal Triumph from the Frontiers of Brain Science*, Norman Doidge explains that our brains learn to adapt, and the brain's very matrix changes with repetitive, colorful, multisensorial exposure. Your brain will collaborate with you to change if you repeatedly expose it to new opportunities and experiences that are associated with the self-culture you are uncovering.

Repetitive meditation and visualization are fundamental techniques for creating new neural pathways and achieving change in your beliefs. In a meditative state, you can visualize yourself living the life you want to live or being in the kind of relationship you wish to be in. When you do this, it is important to make your image as clear, colorful and specific as you can. You can also use other methods to express your vision, such as writing it, speaking it, singing it, acting it, drawing it and incorporating movement with your visualization, such as putting your hand to your heart or interlocking your fingers. Use as many of these as possible; the effect of engaging multiple senses is alchemical and results in greater success in achieving your heart's desire.

The Exercise for Anchoring New Neural Pathways

This wonderful exercise is a way to anchor your new beliefs into your deeper consciousness and core of your being. It's an important exercise to create new neural pathways for anything you'd like to change in your belief system. It's a multilayered method that's done using three techniques at once: visual, auditory and kinesthetic. Don't worry if you don't believe what you are saying, visualizing or doing, just "fake it until you make it!"[1]

You can do this exercise to create new neural pathways and new beliefs about anything; however, I have tailored it here to help you rewire your beliefs and your neural pathways associated with being in relationships.

I recommend that you record the instructions, reading them slowly, so you can have your eyes closed and fully relax while you play it back. Have a pen and paper handy so you can write as well.

Take a moment to sit quietly, close your eyes and do some slow deep breathing for few minutes. Allow yourself to become very relaxed.

---

[1] "Fake it until you make it" derives from the neuro-linguistic programming (NLP) principle that it isn't necessary to understand the hows and whys of what you are doing, but by the law of cause and effect, where like causes produce like effects, by acting a part, you can make it a reality.

1. **Your visual anchor:** Visualize yourself living the life you want to live. (Pause. Breathe.) See yourself in a healthy and happy relationship. (Pause. Breathe.) In this scene, you see yourself feeling safe, joyful, attractive and loved by a wonderful partner. (Pause. Breathe.) See everything in great detail. Get very clear about how you are feeling in this ideal life and relationship. (Pause. Breathe.)

2. **Your auditory anchor:** Take the time to find a clear sentence that truly represents all that you are visualizing. The sentence should be said in the present tense and begin with "I." For example, "I now am able to draw healthy boundaries in my life," or "I now attract only healthy people into my life," or "I am now in a relationship in which I feel joy, love, deep attraction and emotional safety," or "I am now living a life in which I am in a healthy, happy, balanced and sexually fulfilling relationship." (Pause. Breathe. Write the sentence down.) Once you create the right statement or two, please close your eyes again and breathe slowly. Then say the sentence(s) out loud a few times. Continue to visualize the scene while saying the sentence(s).

3. **Your kinesthetic anchor:** While you say your sentence(s) and visualize your scene, make a movement; for example, put your hand to your heart or interlace your fingers and place them on your chest or do the "cross crawl," in which you lift your left knee to your right elbow and then lift your right knee to your left elbow, and then repeat the sequence for about twenty seconds, all the while still visualizing and saying the sentence(s).

When you do all three at the same time, you drive your new beliefs deeper into your consciousness, which makes the new neural pathways thicker and, therefore, your new behavior patterns easier to maintain.

Selected Bibliography

Beattie, Melody. *Codependent No More: How to Stop Controlling Others and Start Caring for Yourself.* Center City, MN: Hazelden Foundation, 1992.

Beattie, Melody. *Codependents' Guide to the Twelve Steps: How to Find the Right Program for You and Apply Each of the Twelve Steps to Your Own Issues.* New York: Fireside, 1990.

Brown, Brené. *Daring Greatly: How the Courage to Be Vulnerable Transforms the Way We Live, Love, Parent, and Lead.* New York: Gotham Books, 2012.

Carter, Steven, and Julia Sokol. *He's Scared, She's Scared: Understanding the Hidden Fears That Sabotage Your Relationships.* New York: Dell Publishing, 1993.

Chapman, Gary. *The 5 Love Languages: The Secret to Love That Lasts.* Chicago: Northfield Publishing, 2015.

Coelho, Paulo. *The Alchemist: A Fable about Following Your Dream.* San Francisco: HarpersCollins, 1993.

Doidge, Norman. *The Brain That Changes Itself: Stories of Personal Triumph from the Frontiers of Brain Science.* London: Penguin Books, 2007.

Easton, Dossie, and Catherine A. Liszt. *The Ethical Slut: A Guide to Infinite Sexual Possibilities.* San Francisco: Greenery Press, 1997.

Gilbert, Roberta M. *Extraordinary Relationships: A New Way of Thinking about Human Interactions.* New York: John Wiley & Sons, 1992.

Gottman, John M., and Nan Silver. *The Seven Principles for Making Marriage Work: A Practical Guide from the Country's Foremost Relationship Expert.* New York: Harmony Books, 2015.